THE COMMODITIES INVESTOR

A beginner's guide to diversifying your portfolio with commodities

Philip Scott

HARRIMAN HOUSE LTD

3A Penns Road
Petersfield
Hampshire
GU32 2EW
GREAT BRITAIN

Tel: +44 (0)1730 233870
Fax: +44 (0)1730 233880
Email: enquiries@harriman-house.com
Website: www.harriman-house.com

First published in Great Britain in 2010
Copyright © Harriman House Ltd

The right of Philip Scott to be identified as Author has been asserted in accordance
with the Copyright, Design and Patents Act 1988.

ISBN: 978-1905641-83-3

British Library Cataloguing in Publication Data
A CIP catalogue record for this book can be obtained from the British Library.

Printed and bound by the CPI Group Antony Rowe, Chippenham

For Ella

Contents

Acknowledgements

I would like to thank Harriman House for their assistance and support, especially Stephen Eckett, Craig Pearce and Myles Hunt.

And to the following individuals for extending their time, knowledge and research: Emma Phillips and the commodities team at BlackRock, Nicholas Brookes at ETF Securities, Barclays Capital, Ian Henderson at J.P. Morgan Asset Management, Mick Gilligan at Killik & Co, Mark Dampier, Ben Yearsley, and Meera Patel at Hargreaves Lansdown, Justin Urquhart Stewart at Seven Investment Management, and Darius McDermott at Chelsea Financial Services.

I would also like to thank Andrew Oxlade, Adrian Lowery, Ed Monk, Simon Lambert, Richard Browning, James Hicking, Alan O'Sullivan, Gillian Bevis and T. Evans as well as Simon Moon and Richard Dyson, Jo Thornhill, Toby Walne and Helen Loveless at the *Financial Mail*.

I would also like to thank Karen Wagg, Justin Modray, Anna Bowes, Vanessa Chance, Katie Hayward, Kevin Carr, Alison Merrigan, Lyndsay Haywood, Paul Gosker, Ian Patterson, Johanna Gornitzki, Nicole Blackmore, Jo Fox, James Smith, Paul Shaffer, Catherine Barnett, Francesca Pattison and Justine Fisher, Charles and Sarah Scott, Des Scott and Judy Abassi, John Lappin, Nicola York, James Salmon, Sam Shaw, Amanda Smith, James Phillipps and Gregor Watt.

And special thanks to Jenne Mannion, Susie Tempest, Gerry K. Glennon, Barbara J. Walshe, George and Julia Stuart, and Elizabeth Grace and Dominic Green.

Preface

What the book covers

This book deals with investing in commodities – the resources of the world. It examines what is involved when it comes to investing in this unique but volatile asset class.

An in-depth look is taken at the major resources within the energy, precious metals, industrial metals and agricultural sectors, including:

Energy	Precious Metals	Industrial Metals	Agriculture
Oil	Gold	Aluminium	Corn
Natural gas	Platinum	Copper	Soybeans
	Palladium	Nickel	Wheat
	Silver	Zinc	

Each section outlines what investors need to know: the basic information for each commodity, the performance history and the outlook for the future are examined, as well as the easiest ways in which to invest.

The investment vehicles referenced in this book are typically funds that have been mentioned, as expert recommendations, on a number of occasions when I have been writing about commodities as a journalist. I have chosen to focus on funds and exchange traded funds/exchange traded commodities as the main means of investing as I believe they are the simplest, most cost-efficient route for investors into the world of commodities. They are an ideal way of creating a diversified commodity portfolio.

Some of the funds here may invest in just one area, for example in energy related stocks, which could include investments in the shares of companies involved in the oil and natural gas industries. The majority of funds, however, will have a spread of investments across commodities – they will have exposure to areas such as agriculture, base metals, precious metals and energy investments.

Who the book is for

The book is written for individuals who already have some experience of investing but are looking at new ways in which to expand and diversify their portfolios – in this case, with commodities. It may also be of potential interest to those who have not yet invested at all, but are keen to learn about investing in commodities and the driving forces behind the world of resources.

The book should be treated as an introduction to the world of investing in commodities – its aim is to explain the long-term prospects for the commodities, in broad terms. Successful investing should always be regarded as a long-term strategy (five to ten years at least) and as such this book is not designed for short-term traders.

How the book is structured

The book starts by describing the macro view of commodities and why they are such big news. It also has a detailed description of what type of funds you can use to gain exposure to this asset class as well as guidance on investing.

The main part of the book looks at the most important commodities within the four major resource sectors: energy, precious metals, agriculture and industrial metals. Each section contains an overview of each sector, dedicated individual chapters on each commodity covered and then sections on how to invest. The commodities highlighted are those which have tended to dominate the headlines and investor interest in recent years – with oil and gold being obvious examples.

So for example, the energy section of the book contains a macro-overview of the sector, which is followed by individual and detailed chapters on oil and natural gas. These chapters are then followed by a section on how you can best invest in the energy sector. The sections on precious metals, industrial metals and agriculture follow the same structure.

A note on price charts

Throughout this book charts showing the price history of commodities and indices are used. Unless otherwise stated, commodities are represented on the charts by a thick line, and the FTSE 100 index is represented by a thin, dashed line.

INTRODUCTION

The Commodities Super Cycle

In 1998 Jim Rogers, ex-partner of George Soros, began talking about the potential for commodities. Commodity prices were then at low levels not seen since the Great Depression and, according to Rogers, the time had come to invest in them.

But at the time the world wasn't interested. People wanted to talk about Worldcom, Enron and Pets.com. However, over the following decade commodity prices soared, outperforming by a wide margin equities, bonds and most other asset classes.

This boom in commodity prices came to be called the Commodity Super Cycle. Jim Rogers says that commodity cycles have historically lasted 15 years, and as this current cycle started around 2000 we're still in the middle of it.[1] In fact, in October 2009 Rogers said:

> I don't see any adequate supply situation in any commodity market over the next decade or two. The commodities boom is not over and the bull market has several years to go.[2]

---

[1] http://treasurepicks.blogspot.com/2008/01/commodity-bull-jim-rogers-says-super.html

[2] http://www.telegraph.co.uk/finance/newsbysector/industry/6276453/Jim-Rogers-predicts-that-commodities-boom-could-last-20-years.html

There are two fundamental factors that are seen as the drivers of this Super Cycle.

The first is the expected growth of the world's population. At the moment, the globe's population is growing at a rate of 76m people annually; by 2050 the population is forecast to be 9.1bn (up from 6.5bn today). Not only are the raw numbers increasing but consumption patterns are changing. For example, as people in emerging markets become richer they consume more; they buy cars and change their eating habits to more resource-intensive diets. Such a growing population in a world of finite raw materials will lead to an upward pressure on commodity prices.

" Commodities can play a useful role in a well-diversified portfolio. "

The second factor is increasing infrastructure spending by emerging markets. Emerging economies, especially China and India, are set to consume vast resources on infrastructure developments. China already consumes more copper, steel and iron ore than the United States and Japan combined.

Later in this book we will be looking at these factors in more detail, analysing the influences on demand and supply for individual commodities.

The 2007-09 credit crisis hit commodity prices along with most other asset classes. However, most of the fundamentals set to drive commodity prices higher are still in place. And as economies slowly recover, it is likely that demand will outpace supply as the latter is less flexible, and having been wound down as a result of the crisis, supply cannot be increased again at the flick of a switch.

In summary, the outlook for commodities is expected to be good.

However, the message of this book is not, "fill your boots with commodities because they're all going up!" Rather, it is about diversification.

Portfolio diversification

Historically, commodities have not been closely correlated with other asset classes such as equities. When equity markets fall, commodities have tended to rise, and vice versa. Admittedly, during the 2007-09 credit crisis the prices of pretty much all asset classes – including commodities – fell. But that was an extreme situation. In normal circumstances commodities and equities are not closely correlated and it is likely that that long-established relationship will re-assert itself.

As such, commodities can play a useful role in a well-diversified portfolio. This is not to suggest that a significant proportion of a portfolio should be in commodities, but a level of around 5% (or 10% for the more aggressive portfolios) would seem to be reasonable.

The problem until recently has been that investing in commodities was not at all easy. One could trade commodities for the short-term with, say, futures, but holding long-term positions was difficult for all investors, whether they were private investors or professionals.

Fortunately, the situation has recently changed dramatically with the introduction of exchange traded commodities.

Exchange traded commodities

Exchange traded commodities listed on exchanges – such as the London Stock Exchange – have made long-term investments in commodities easily accessible to all investors. With these new instruments, adding wheat to an investment portfolio is as simple as adding Vodafone.

Of course, these exchange traded funds can be used for more than just portfolio diversification; they can also be used for speculation and hedging. As an example of the latter, if you are worried about the future cost of fuel (for cars or heating) your future expenses can now be hedged directly with the purchase of an exchange traded fund linked to the price of Brent Crude oil.

This book looks at other ways to gain exposure to commodities, such as OEICs (open ended investment companies) and investment trusts, but it is primarily these exchange traded commodities that will be the focus. They are, without hyperbole, revolutionary and can change the investing world for all investors.

Commodities: The Big Picture

Historic price performance

In recent years, the commodity story reached epic proportions. Rising demand, limited supply and volatile stock markets all coincided to drive up the price of resources and agricultural commodities across the globe. This perfect storm – soaring demand for everything from oil to gold, from corn to natural gas – sent markets, investors and the media into a frenzy. The demand for resources, especially from the vast populations of the world's emerging economies, such as China and India, was insatiable.

In March 2008 gold broke through the US$1000 an ounce barrier for the first time. The prices of other precious metals, such as platinum, also soared. And agricultural commodities such as soybeans and corn scaled new heights.

But economies worldwide slowed following the credit crunch and commodity prices fell along with other assets such as equities and property.

Commodities and inflation

➤ Commodities tend to be positively correlated with inflation.

➤ Bonds and equities tend to be negatively correlated with inflation.

➤ Commodities therefore provide an inflation hedge as well as diversification benefits.

Figure 1 shows an index of commodity prices, illustrating how prices peaked in 2008 and then fell back sharply.

Figure 1: index of commodity prices (1999-2009)

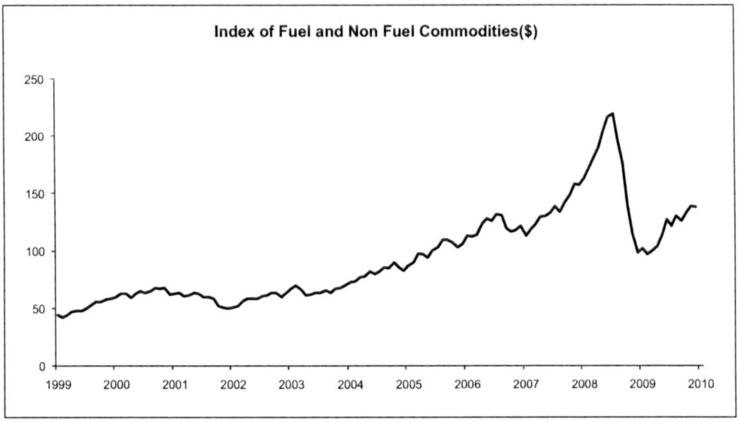

Source: IMF

During the commodity boom many made a fortune while others, too over-exposed to commodities, lost one. Commodities, then, are a volatile investment class.

Oil can be taken as an example of this volatility. In the middle of 2007, just prior to the commencement of the credit crunch, oil was hovering around US$70 a barrel. Fast-forward 12 months and the price of oil had doubled to hit record highs. And yet a few months later oil was trading under US$40.

Comparative performance

During the financial crisis of 2008 and 2009 commodity prices tumbled alongside shares, but this was unusual. As mentioned earlier, commodities tend not to be correlated with other assets and generally when stocks do well, commodities tend to fall back, and vice versa. During the 1980s and 1990s, for example, share markets performed well but commodities were left behind.

Figure 2 shows the comparative performance of an index of commodities (in sterling terms) with the FTSE 100 Index (the values have been re-based to start at 100 to allow for easy comparison).

Figure 2: index of commodity prices v FTSE 100 Index (1999-2009)

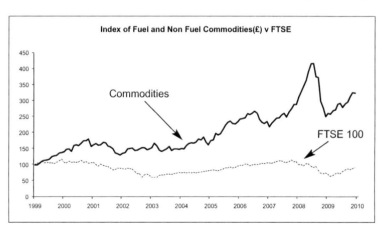

Source: IMF

From January 1999 to December 2009 the FTSE 100 fell 8.2%, while over the same period the commodity index increased 223%.

It's not perfect, but a cursory analysis of Figure 2 shows that equities and commodities have not been closely correlated – which supports the argument that commodities can offer useful diversification for an equity investor.

The outlook for commodities

Commodities did not have much attention bestowed upon them during the last 20 years of the 20th century. But that has changed dramatically in the last few years. The importance of the resource boom witnessed in this last decade can most easily be understood when you look at what's going on in the world's emerging economies.

Jim O'Neill, of investment banking giant Goldman Sachs, coined the term BRIC, an acronym for the emerging markets of Brazil, Russia, China and India. By 2050 it is forecast that only the United States and Japan will remain in G7, the group of the world's seven richest nations; taking over from the UK, Germany, Italy and France will be the BRICs.

> **The importance of the BRICs, especially China, will be obvious when reading this book.**

Brazil is blessed with vast natural resources, such as iron ore; India is emerging as an important nation in global outsourcing; Russia is a dominant player in the energy commodities of oil and gas; and China's growth (where the economy has typically been expanding by around 9% each year since 1980) is being powered by its industrial strength.

The importance of the BRICs, especially China, will be obvious as you read further. And as the BRICs prosper, consumer spending in these countries will rise – over the coming decades these four developing nations could potentially deliver another 1.8bn consumers.

More mouths to feed – the effect on agricultural commodities

In 1999, the world's population surpassed 6bn – a 300% rise in a century. According to the United Nations, every year there are 78m more mouths to feed – providing a rapidly expanding market at a time when global food stocks are at historically low levels. It has been estimated that by 2030 there could potentially be over 8bn people inhabiting the planet.

As well as more food being needed to feed growing populations, people in emerging markets are enjoying greater affluence as a result of their expanding economies. This means these vast populations are eating more meat, such as beef. A rise in demand for beef means an increase in demand for cattle, and with it a larger requirement for animal feed, such as corn, soybeans and wheat.

With this in mind, it is not surprising that Jim Rogers has stated a bull market in commodities could continue for another 15 years. He said:

> Wheat, soya, maize and orange juice are all far below their all-time highs. There will be fortunes made in agriculture in the next decade.

It should also be considered that agricultural commodities are not just used for food – their use in 'green' fuel alternatives should further augment the bull market. A report from the Renewable Fuels Commission pointed out that an unchecked push for biofuels could increase food prices significantly in the short to medium term.

Infrastructure demands – the effect on industrial metal commodities

Commodity demand will also be driven by the development and urbanisation of economies like China and India.

For commodities such as copper, lead, tin and aluminium, demand should be strong over the long term. Demand for steel and raw materials for steelmaking is dominated by China and the developing world. In China the amount of money scheduled to be spent on railways is huge – spending has been increased five-fold to £16bn a year.

In India, the planning commission estimates that about £300bn needs to be invested in infrastructure over the coming years, while a further £150bn is needed in the corporate sector to build more factories and offices. Better wages also mean a potentially huge growth in spending on cars – which will increase demand for fuel, biofuel, platinum and base metals such as aluminium.

In the Western world too, lacklustre economic performance and privatisation from the mid-1970s to the mid-1990s caused 20 years of underinvestment and a need to revamp crumbling infrastructure.

Supply constraints

While demand for commodities is likely to remain strong, there are various production constraints that could lead to disruptions in supply – and therefore an increase in prices.

For many years there was underinvestment in developing new mines. That may be changing slowly now, but it can take many years for production to come on stream from new mines.

The political situation in commodity-producing countries has an impact too. For example, civil unrest in Kenya, the world's largest supplier of black tea, has previously led to obstructive market conditions. Instability in the Ivory Coast, the world's largest cocoa producer, has also caused problems.

Summary

Arguably, a great attribute of commodities is that they are not complicated – the need for them is obvious. Unlike, say, the mania around complicated and misunderstood technology investments at the turn of the century, commodities are the lifeblood of planet earth, they help to build, power and feed the globe. And generally demand is outstripping supply – in some cases significantly so. In light of all this, the forecast is that commodities, despite fluctuations and setbacks, should yield positive returns over the long term.

Commodities outlook: key points

➤ Emerging economies such as China and India are consuming large quantities of raw commodities.

➤ Rising incomes mean more demand for high protein diets.

➤ Hard commodities are finite and the easy, cheap resources have been mined.

➤ World inventories for many agricultural commodities are at historic lows and the global population is rising.

➤ Capital expenditure and discoveries may take years to catch up.

➤ A negative or uncertain outlook for other asset classes has historically been good for commodities.

.

Investing In Commodities

Investing in commodities is not an activity for widows or orphans.

These are high-risk investments, often experiencing high volatility. So even the most intrepid of investors should only hold a small proportion of commodity investments in their portfolio, around 5%, or maybe 10% if they can afford to and are comfortable with the risks involved.

How to access the commodities markets

If you want to invest in commodities there are several ways to do it. I explain the main alternatives below.

Commodity exposure in the FTSE 100 Index

Many companies in the FTSE 100 already have exposure to commodity prices – and this has been increasing in recent years. Such firms include BHP Billiton, Xstrata, Eurasian Natural Resources, Kazakhmys and Vedanta Resources, as well as BP and Shell. So any diversification into commodities should take account of existing exposure either through direct investment in these companies or funds that track the FTSE 100.

Direct

The obvious direct investment is to buy the physical commodity. For example, in the case of gold this would mean buying bullion. Of course if you buy bullion or any physical commodity, which can be done through dedicated dealers, you need to remember that you will have to pay extra costs to store it in a suitable deposit (unless you are happy to keep it under your bed). While it is feasible to buy gold bullion, buying other commodities is rarely practical, so we do not look at this any further except in the case of precious metals.

Futures and options

It is possible to trade futures (and options) on a range of commodities.[3] A list of traded commodity futures can be seen at http://en.wikipedia.org/wiki/List_of_traded_commodities, and a table of the latest commodity futures prices can be found at http://money.cnn.com/data/commodities.

However, futures are not necessarily suitable for long-term holdings and they require a level of knowledge beyond that assumed in this book, so futures and options are not covered.

Spread betting and CFDs

There are spread bet and CFD contracts linked to commodities. However, like futures, these are not really suitable for long term-investors and so are not covered in this book.

Equities

A way of getting exposure to commodities is through buying shares in companies involved in the exploration, development, processing or mining of commodities. For example, to get exposure to gold one could buy shares in Cluff Gold. Buying Royal Dutch Shell would give exposure to the oil price, Antofagasta would give exposure to copper and New Britain Palm Oil gives exposure to palm oil. (All companies mentioned are listed on the London Stock Exchange.)

When this works, it can work very well as often the company's profits are a geared play on the commodity price – in other words, if the commodity

---

[3] But not, bizarrely, onions in the United States – the 1958 Onion Futures Act bans the trading of futures contracts on onions!

price increases by 5% this can lead to a much greater increase in the company profits (and therefore also a magnified rise in the share price).

But it's not always as easy as that.

Share prices are influenced by many factors, such as the peculiarities of the company itself, the sentiment in the market as a whole and the outlook for the economy. In some cases, commodity producers may hedge their future earnings by selling forward their production at a price fixed today – the result being that the company may not benefit if the commodity price subsequently soars (this has happened in the past with some gold miners).

Take a look at Figure 3. It compares the share price of Cluff Gold with the gold price (in sterling).[4]

Figure 3: Cluff Gold v Gold(£)

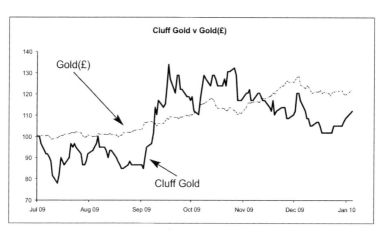

As can be seen, the sterling price of gold increased steadily in the second half of 2009, but the share price of Cluff Gold was all over the place. One can spot some periods of slight correlation, but overall it could not be said that the two were closely correlated. As such, if one had invested in Cluff Gold shares to give exposure to gold, one might have been disappointed.

---

[4] The charts have been rebased to start at 100 to enable them to be displayed on the same chart.

To summarise, shares can sometimes be an excellent geared play on related commodity prices, but the influences on share prices are complex. Investing in individual shares to give exposure to commodities is therefore a sophisticated activity and beyond the scope of this book. However, we will be looking at investing in funds of shares to spread the risk.

So far, futures, options, spread betting, CFDs and individual equities have been dismissed as suitable vehicles for investors to gain exposure to commodities. I could go on. Covered warrants and binary betting are also not considered as suitable for commodity investors for the purposes of this book.

Having dismissed all these – what's left?

We now get to the heart of what this book is about: investing in commodities through funds and, especially, ETFs.

Funds

As mentioned above, investing in individual equities to gain exposure to specific commodities is not simple. So we will instead concentrate on investing in funds of equities that have commodity exposure; unit trusts, OEICs and investment trusts.

Unit trusts and OEICs can be bought direct from a fund manager or from a funds supermarket. Investment trusts are listed on the London Stock Exchange and can be bought and sold like any ordinary share.

Just to be clear, the majority of funds referred to as commodity funds do not invest directly in commodities themselves, but rather in companies that have exposure one way or another to commodities.

In the last few years a new type of fund has appeared that has proven very popular. These are exchange traded funds (ETFs). These funds have transformed the investing world for many investors – including investors in commodities. They are so important, and they play such an important role in this book, that we will now spend some time looking at what ETFs are and the important points investors in ETFs have to bear in mind.

Exchange traded funds (ETFs)

ETFs originated in the United States – the first was launched in 1993, and was based on the American S&P 500 index. They were introduced to Europe in 2000. According to Hargreaves Lansdown, there is now more than €85bn invested in over 400 ETFs in Europe. One ETF, called **Gold Bullion Securities** (that tracks the price of gold), now holds over 100 tonnes of gold with a value over US$4bn.

The purpose of ETFs is to track the performance of a particular market or index, such as the FTSE 100. Like a traditional tracker, the aim is for the ETF to closely follow the performance of the target index. For example, if the FTSE 100 increases 5.1% over a particular period then the price of a FTSE 100 ETF should also rise 5.1%.

ETFs differ from traditional tracker funds in that they are traded like individual stocks, on an exchange such as the London Stock Exchange, and can be bought and sold through brokers in the same way as any other listed stocks during the trading day.

An ETF is what is often referred to as a *passive investment* in that it is not actively managed by a fund manager – a professional who chooses which assets to buy and sell. An ETF merely reflects the movements of the particular index it follows and it only trades in the market to reflect structural changes in the index.

Among the main issuers of ETFs are Deutsche Bank (www.dbxtrackers.co.uk), iShares (www.ishares.co.uk) and Lyxor (www.lyxoretf.co.uk).

The ETF revolution has opened up a whole new universe of choice to investors at a low cost. They allow easy access to foreign indices (e.g. Korea or Turkey), to groups of countries (e.g. BRICs), to investment themes (e.g. global clean energy), to bonds and also to commodities.

Exchange traded commodities (ETCs)

The world's first commodity ETF was the **Gold Bullion Securities** listed on the Australian Stock Exchange in 2003. The first oil ETF was launched in 2005 by ETF Securities – the **ETFS Brent Oil**.

There are now many ETFs that track commodity prices. These commodity ETFs now tend to be called exchange traded commodities (ETCs). ETFs and ETCs are very similar (and the terms ETF and ETC are used interchangeably in this book), however, there is one area – that of regulation – where the difference should be noted.

Ben Yearsley of Hargreaves Lansdown says:

> In the past, investors have had to purchase shares in commodity companies such as Rio Tinto in order to gain exposure to commodities. Whilst this does provide exposure, it is an indirect exposure which means that the commodity company's share price can still fall even if the commodity in question actually rises in value. ETCs now provide investors with direct access and exposure to these commodities and with that the ability to further diversify their portfolios.

To date, apart from ETCs for gold, nearly all ETCs have been issued by ETF Securities (www.etfsecurities.com).

A comprehensive table of all ETCs listed on the London Stock Exchange can be found in the appendix.

Tracking

The first ETCs that tracked gold were backed by holdings in the physical commodity and still today there are listed ETCs for gold, silver, platinum and palladium that are backed by holdings of physical precious metals. You can even arrange for delivery of the metal bullion if you wish.

However, most ETCs are backed by holdings in commodity futures contracts. The reason is that long-term holdings can be difficult to arrange in some commodities (i.e. some agricultural commodities would decay), and futures provide a method for standardisation of pricing (with agricultural commodities prices can vary by season and region). The significance of this is that the ETCs do not directly track the commodity price, but rather they track an index of the commodity.

For example, the coffee ETC tracks the DJ-UBS Coffee Sub-Index[SM] – an index compiled by Dow Jones-UBS.[5] And this index is based on the coffee futures contracts traded on NYBOT.

The obvious question is: how closely do these indexes of futures contracts follow the price of the physical commodity? The answer is: quite closely, but there is a difference.

The principal reason why there is a difference is rollover cost. Futures contracts only have a limited life (often 1-3 months), so maintaining a long-term position in futures requires the frequent selling of expiring contracts and buying of new ones. Such an action incurs a cost. The tracking error is unfortunate; but this is the price to be paid for the convenience of these ETCs.

Credit risk

Related to the foregoing discussion on tracking error, is the issue of counterparty risk. Holding bullion in a bank is one thing, but an ETC backed by a portfolio of futures contracts suggests a different sort of credit exposure. ETF Securities cut to the chase in the FAQ section on their website with the question:

What would happen if ETF Securities were to go bankrupt?

They answer:

> If ETF Securities were to go bankrupt, this would not affect the value of the ETCs. Each ETC is issued by a Special Purpose Vehicle whose assets are ring-fenced for investors' safety and the activities for each Issuer are monitored by an independent Trustee. ETF Securities does not hold any investor money at any time.

---

[5] Further information can be found at www.djindexes.com.

So, much depends on these Special Purpose Vehicles (SPVs). For example, ETF Securities' agricultural ETFs are issued by an SPV called ETFS Commodity Securities Ltd., while their oil ETFs are issued by ETFS Oil Securities Ltd.

It is beyond the scope of this book to go into great detail on credit risk, but for investors wanting to know more, there is further information on the ETF Securities website.

Regulation

Technically, ETCs use a secured, undated, zero coupon note structure. It's not necessary to understand everything about that to invest in ETCs, but it is useful to know that – unlike ETFs – ETCs are not strictly funds. And because ETCs are not a fund structure, and the ETF Securities' SPVs are incorporated in Jersey, it means they are not part of the FSCS compensation scheme and ETF Securities is regulated by the Jersey Financial Services Commission.

Currency exposure

Most commodities are priced in US Dollars, which means that an investor investing in commodities has exposure to:

1. fluctuations in the commodity price, *and*

2. fluctuations in the exchange rate (for a sterling-based investor, this would be the GBP/USD exchange rate).

Most ETCs are priced in dollars, but some are priced in sterling. For example, there are two Gold Bullion Securities:

1. the **Gold Bullion Securities** denominated in US Dollars (TIDM code: GBS)

2. the **Gold Bullion Securities** denominated in sterling (TIDM code: GBSS)

The key thing to note is that the denomination of the ETC does not change the currency exposure (which is to the currency of the underlying commodity). Just because the GBSS ETC is priced in sterling does not remove the exposure to the US Dollar, and investment in either GBS or GBSS will result in the same return.

Costs

One of the main attractions of ETFs is their low cost.

➤ **Commissions**: the cost of trading ETFs is the same as that for any share listed on the LSE and will depend on your broker. Commissions can be £10 or lower per trade. This is much less than would be incurred for most funds.

➤ **Management fees**: annual fees (sometimes referred as TER – total expense ratio) for commodity ETFs are typically around 0.50%. Again, this is much lower than for other funds (where TERs of 1.5% are common).

ISAs or SIPPs

Most ETCs are eligible investments for ISAs and SIPPs in the UK.

Stamp duty

ETCs are not liable for stamp duty in the UK.

ETC variations

Beyond plain vanilla ETCs (e.g. a wheat ETC), there is now a wide range of more complex ETCs:

➤ **Leveraged**: A leveraged ETF accentuates the fluctuations in the commodity price. It may be designed to change by two times the percentage change of a commodity price.

➤ **Forward**: These ETCs track futures with different maturities (e.g. ETFS Brent 1yr tracks the performance of the Brent futures contracts with a 1-year maturity).

➤ **Short**: These are for bearish investors who believe a commodity is going to fall in value.

Readers may be relieved to know that none of these advanced ETCs are essential for the commodity investor and so will not be mentioned any further in this book.

Commodity baskets

As well as ETCs that are linked to single commodities there are also ETCs linked to baskets (or indexes) of commodities. Some examples are:

➤ **ETFS Industrial Metals DJ-UBSCI**ᴿᴹ: an ETC designed to track the basket of industrial metal commodities of aluminium, copper, zinc and nickel.

➤ **ETFS Energy DJ-UBSCI**ˢᴹ: a basket ETC tracking crude oil, natural gas, unleaded gasoline and heating oil.

➤ **ETFS Grains DJ-UBSCI**ˢᴹ: a basket ETC tracking soybeans, corn and wheat.

➤ **ETFS All Commodities DJ-UBSCI**ˢᴹ: basket ETC tracking, well, just about everything – energy, precious metals, industrial metals, livestock and agriculture.

Such basket ETCs can be useful for investors who just want to hold one or two ETCs but with a wide exposure to commodities, or for investors with limited funds who cannot afford to diversify sufficiently with holdings in a number of individual ETCs.

A comprehensive list of these basket ETCs can be found in the appendix.

Risk

A final note on risk. As this section mentioned at the beginning, investing in commodities is not for widows or orphans. The volatility of commodity prices can be high, which makes them risky. One way to reduce risk is to diversify – an ETC which follows just corn will be more risky than a basket ETC which tracks soybeans and wheat as well as corn, as your risk is spread across three markets

Further information

Before investing in any ETC it is wise to inform yourself fully on its details. The first thing to do is to visit the website of the ETC provider (this will usually be ETF Securities, www.etfsecurities.com) and download the factsheet. The types of things you should check are:

➤ *Exactly what does the ETC track?* For example, the **ETFS Industrial Metals DJ-UBSCI**^{SM} tracks a basket of aluminium, copper, zinc and nickel, but the basket does not hold those metals in equal proportions (e.g. 37% of the basket is copper). Make sure you know what the ETC tracks and you are happy with this.

➤ *How is the ETC hedged?* Does the ETC hold the underlying commodity directly (e.g. gold bullion in the case of **Gold Bullion Securities**), or does it hold a portfolio of futures contracts (e.g. the method used for most non-precious metal ETCs)?

➤ *Who is the issuer of the ETC?* For example, the ETFS Brent 1mth ETC is issued by ETFS Oil Securities Ltd. – a Special Purpose Vehicle used by ETF Securities.

➤ *Where is the primary listing?* You will want to check this is the London Stock Exchange.

➤ *What is the exchange code for the ETC?* For example, the exchange code (called TIDM on the LSE) for the **ETFS Industrial Metals DJ-UBSCI**^{SM} is AIGIP.

➤ *What is the annual management fee?* As mentioned, ETC management fees are generally lower than for other types of funds, but you will still want to check how the management fee for the ETC you are considering will affect the returns of your investment.

Key points: ETCs

➤ An easy way to gain direct access to commodity prices. ETCs are listed on the London Stock Exchange and can be traded like any share.

➤ Very wide range of ETCs available allowing for very precise exposure to commodities to be constructed.

➤ Low cost. Dealing fees and TER are low relative to most funds.

➤ No stamp duty.

ENERGY **A**

Introduction

Energy commodities – of which we shall concentrate on crude oil and natural gas – provide fuel for industry, transport, and heating or cooling buildings. Issues surrounding these commodities are highly political, and the influences on their prices widespread, because of their importance for developing and sustaining economic growth.

We will now look into the demand, supply and outlook for oil and natural gas, followed by advice on what investing options are available.

OIL | 1

The raw material crude oil is refined to produce gasoline, heating oil, diesel and aviation fuel. It is a versatile and portable energy source, which powers the vast majority of the planet's vehicles, and it is the base for a large number of industrial chemicals. The central place that oil occupies within everyday life means that when the price rises it places severe pressure on households, motorists and businesses. Such is its importance that it has earned the sobriquet 'black gold'.

Perhaps the most fundamental consideration for the long term is the self-evident fact that oil is a fossil fuel and reserves will one day run out. This suggests that unless demand decreases – and taking into account the rapid industrialisation of such countries as India and China this seems unlikely – oil is to become increasingly precious in the medium to long term.

Oil has traditionally had a low correlation with equities, meaning that an investment in oil can add useful diversification to your portfolio. However, it is worth bearing in mind that you may already

> **Oil traditionally has a low correlation with equities.**

have exposure to oil through other UK investments. For instance, investors who have shares in an equity fund will most likely be invested in companies that mine or distribute oil.

Price performance

An important landmark was when oil reached US$100 a barrel in early 2008 – the spike was spurred on partly by a languishing US dollar, geopolitical tensions in Kenya, Pakistan and Algeria, as well as the threat of coercion against Iran by the United States. These events were contemporaneous with significant concern over a winter fuel supply shortfall and speculators were also thought to be active in driving up the price.

Looking at Figure 4, the most significant event in the last ten years is this price spike in 2008, and the subsequent correction. In June 2008, West Texas oil reached nearly $134 a barrel, but six months later it was trading at $41 – a fall in price of nearly 70%. This example illustrates how volatile oil can be.

Figure 4: oil price (1999-2009)

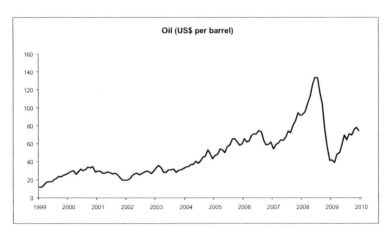

Source: IMF

In the period 1999-2009, an investment in oil would have offered a better return than an investment in the FTSE 100 (Figure 5). The oil price increased by 500% in this period – from $12 a barrel in January 1999 to $74 a barrel in December 2009 – while the FTSE recorded an 8% drop. In the last five years the oil price increased by 72%, while the FTSE increased by 12%.

Figure 5: oil price (sterling) v FTSE 100 Index, rebased to 100 (1999-2009)

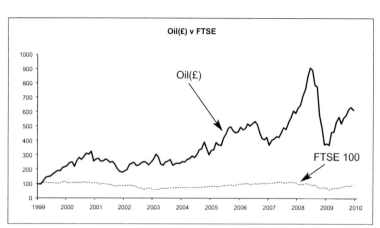

Source: IMF

Let's take a look at some incidents that have affected the oil price in the past.

Historical price volatility of oil – factors that can affect the oil price

A cursory glance at events over recent history paints a stark picture of oil's price volatility and its importance as the chief global source of fuel.

For example, in 1973, as a result of the war between Arab and Israeli forces, OPEC (see p. 32) established an oil embargo in which it declared that it would limit or cut off the supply of oil to the United States and other countries that supported Israel in the war. This caused prices to soar by 400% in just six months.

The combination of the Iranian revolution and the Iran-Iraq war caused crude oil prices to more than double from $14 in 1978 to $35 in 1981. After the Gulf War crude oil prices entered a period of continuous decline, ultimately hitting their lowest levels for 21 years in 1994.

At the turn of the century prices again declined as Russia upped its oil production and the United States' economy went into freefall. OPEC attempted to control production but the terrorist attacks on the United States on 11 September 2001 caused prices to plummet and by mid-November prices were down by some 35%. OPEC pulled back, cutting production again until early 2002 when prices began to rise.

What is OPEC?

OPEC, the Organization of the Petroleum Exporting Countries, is an intergovernmental organisation that was created at the Baghdad Conference in 1960 by Iran, Iraq, Kuwait, Saudi Arabia and Venezuela, to coordinate the oil production policies of its members. The aim is to keep the oil market stable and to help oil producers achieve a reasonable rate of return on their investments.

Its member countries produce about 40% of the world's crude oil (and 15% of its natural gas). However, OPEC's oil exports represent about 55% of the oil traded internationally.

As an investor in oil, announcements from OPEC regarding production should be monitored – these can affect the oil price because of the large concentration of reserves in these countries.

The United States-led invasion of Iraq in 2003 caused a slowing of oil production there and by mid-2003 the six million barrels a day production had fallen back to below two million, a level which continued over the following two years.

In 2008 accusations were levelled at speculators, such as hedge fund managers, for pushing up the price to new heights. In response to this, OPEC secretary general, Abdalla El-Badri, said that global supply was comfortable and he rejected calls from Britain and Japan to boost output. He pointed to the weak US dollar and speculators as being the primary causes for the high price.

Demand for oil

It has been argued that the record high oil prices of 2008 were evidence of a price bubble, and were the result of speculation by investors – and not the result of true supply and demand forces.[6] It would be of some comfort if the upward trajectory of the oil price was solely the result of speculation, but supply has been relatively stable over the past decade and demand has been rising, which would suggest the availability of the physical commodity is definitely a factor in its rising price.

The countries where demand is expected to increase most are India and China. Per capita oil consumption in Asia is still low compared to the United States and the Middle East but, because of India and China's large and rapidly growing populations, small per capita increases in demand have the potential to have a substantial impact on global demand. As emerging nations develop and continue to industrialise, demand for oil in these countries should rise. Robin Batchelor, fund manager of BlackRock's World Energy Fund, noted that if:

> " As emerging nations develop and continue to industrialise, demand for oil in these countries should rise. "

> China and India were to increase their consumption per person to current US levels, these two countries alone would require 160m barrels per day, more than twice the world's supply of oil today.

Evidence of this was seen in 2008, when China reported a 7.2% annual increase in oil consumption, the largest of any country. North America should not be forgotten though. The high demand from this region – which still represents 25% of world consumption – means the condition of the United States' economy remains an important consideration for the oil investor.

---

[6] Daniel O'Sullivan, *Petromania* (Harriman House, 2009).

Although most evidence points towards an increase in oil consumption, demand will fluctuate. A genuine slowdown in global consumption as a result of recession, as witnessed in 2008, naturally dampens world energy demand in the short term, as manufacturing and consumer demand for goods and services slows. But in the longer term, as economies recover, it is typical that most nations return to a trend of growth in income and therefore energy demand.

Demand: key points

➤ A decline in economic growth usually translates into a decline in demand for oil, because of its place as the main fuel for industry.

➤ In the long term a continuing rise in demand is anticipated, driven by demand from developing economies.

Supply of oil

Oil is a finite, non-reusable resource – once used, it is gone. Some have argued that the world has already reached the maximum point of oil extraction (otherwise referred to as 'peak oil'), which means that from this point on production rates will be in decline until reserves are exhausted.

However, oil is not going to run out in the short term, and for the moment a drastic shortfall in supply is unlikely. The biggest oil reserves are to be found in the Middle East, North America and Russia, which between them account for more than 75% of the estimated world total, and production news from these regions should be monitored.

❝ Production news from the Middle East, North America and Russia should be monitored. ❞

In recent statements OPEC has shown confidence that supply is in good stead. According to them, improved technology, successful exploration and enhanced recovery have enabled the world to increase its resource base to levels well above the expectations of the past, and this will continue in the coming decades. Positive news has also come from the US Geological Survey. Their estimates of ultimately recoverable reserves have doubled since the early 1980s, from just less than 1.7 trillion barrels to over 3.3 trillion barrels, while at the same time cumulative production has been less than one-third of this increase.

Of course, factors that limit supply should be taken into account. Experts have pointed out that the maximum capacity of refineries places a constriction on supply – meaning that, independent of oil reserve figures, there is a limit to how much output of oil there can be.

Further problems are presented by high oil prices having increased resource nationalism, as oil-rich countries demand a larger share of the industry's profits. Oil production in Russia, for example, has experienced setbacks because the government seized control of the country's assets. Countries such as Venezuela, Nigeria and Kazakhstan, where the domestic political situation is liable to be unstable, cannot be relied upon for a consistent supply.

Supply: key points

➤ Oil is a finite, non-reusable resource, which means reserves will dwindle and run out eventually. It is expected that supply will fall below demand in the coming years unless there is a dramatic rise in the current pace of investment in the industry.

➤ Oil prices can be sensitive to even small perceived shortages and so investors should pay attention to news from suppliers, particularly those in North America, Russia and the Middle East.

Oil outlook

Generally it is accepted that oil demand is high and increasing, and supply is limited, the combination of which would suggest that the price of oil will increase. Investing in oil is not so straightforward though, because there are various factors that play a role in the movement of the price, making it volatile. This volatility of course offers opportunities for investors but, as ever, high volatility means high risk.

Tony Hayward, chief executive of energy giant BP, wrote in the group's Statistical *Review of World Energy 2009*:

> Producers and consumers alike are wondering how to manage the myriad issues around energy, including price volatility, security and climate change.
>
> Our data confirms that the world has enough proved reserves of oil, natural gas and coal to meet the world's needs for decades to come. The challenges the world faces in growing supplies to meet future demand are not below ground, they are above ground. They are human, not geological.

There will of course be ups and downs but ultimately it is expected that energy prices in general look set to remain firm over the long term and any fears regarding a supply disruption could and most likely will send prices higher.

Growth in world energy demand, particularly in the Asia-Pacific region, is expected to accelerate significantly due to the concentrated level of rapidly developing economies there.

India and China are expected to be responsible for most of the world's oil demand growth over the next two decades, according to the International Energy Agency (IEA). Indian oil demand is likely to increase by 3.9% annually until 2030, while it has been estimated that Chinese will rise at 3.5% yearly over the same period.

This compares with just 1% year-on-year oil demand growth for the world as a whole. It is expected that India will going to overtake Japan by 2020 as the third largest oil and gas consumer, and that China will overtake the United States by 2025 to become the world's biggest oil and gas consumer.

The anticipated increase in demand, together with supply constraints, means that oil prices are likely to remain high well into the next decade. Indeed, the International Energy Agency has previously cautioned that demand in emerging markets such as India and China is likely to cause the oil price to rise, and OPEC has previously stated that oil could reach US$200 a barrel.

Outlook: key points

➢ There is significant growing demand from emerging economies, especially China.

➢ A drastic supply shortfall is not anticipated in the short to medium term.

➢ Although the overall trend for oil is expected to be an increasing price, there will still be volatility.

NATURAL GAS | 2

Natural gas is a colourless, odourless substance that can be burned to produce power. It is primarily made up of methane and is extracted from oil and gas fields around the world. It is only recently that methods for obtaining and putting it to use were developed, but the majority of natural gas extracted from under the ground is millions of years old. Its main uses are cooking, heating and the generation of electricity.

As concern over global warming grows, natural gas should receive an increasing amount of attention. This is because it burns cleanly. According to the Energy Saving Trust in the UK, natural gas engines produce around 5% less CO_2 when compared to an equivalent model with a diesel engine and around 20% in comparison with petrol engine equivalents. It also delivers 80% lower nitrous oxide emissions than diesel, as well as zero particulate emissions.

> **"As natural gas is one of a group of fuels, its fortunes have traditionally been linked to those of oil. "**

This position of natural gas as one of a group of fuels means that its fortunes have traditionally been linked to those of oil. If oil becomes expensive, consumers seek cheaper fuel in natural gas, which then increases demand for gas and in turn pushes up its price too. The reverse is true when demand for oil falls – as in the 2007-2009 recession. If oil or other fuels experience a drop in demand, their price can fall and this will be mirrored in the natural gas price.

Price performance

Figure 6 shows that the ten-year performance of the Henry Hub natural gas price has been volatile, punctuated as it is by price peaks in late 2000, 2003, 2005, 2006 and 2008. The 2008 spike – when the price reached $475 per thousand cubic metres in June – is clear evidence of the correlation between oil and natural gas, as oil was experiencing record high prices at the time.

Figure 6: natural gas price (1999-2009)

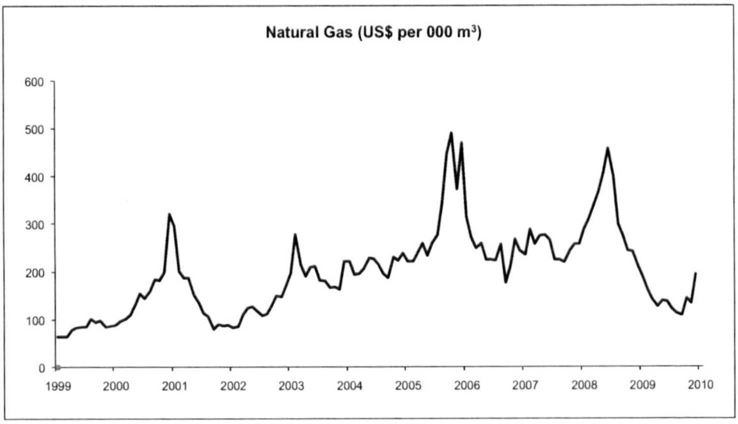

Source: IMF

Henry Hub

Henry Hub is a section of natural gas pipeline in Louisiana which acts as the pricing point for natural gas futures traded on NYMEX.

Between 1999 and 2009 the price of natural gas outperformed the FTSE 100, increasing from $93 to $193 per thousand cubic metres – an increase of 123%. In the last five years natural gas represented a worse investment than the FTSE 100, as its price dropped by 13% while the FTSE rose 12%.

Figure 7: natural gas price (in sterling) v FTSE 100 Index, rebased to 100 (1999-2009)

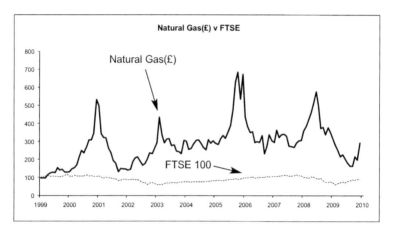

Source: IMF

Demand for natural gas

If oil becomes more expensive and countries seek to reduce their carbon dioxide emissions, natural gas should appear increasingly attractive as an alternative to oil, coal and diesel, and so will be put to wider use.

As with oil, the increasing demand for natural gas from emerging markets – especially China and India – is an important consideration. Currently, these countries are still relatively small consumers of natural gas but demand is on the up – both countries are rapidly expanding infrastructure and gas is an important energy resource in this process. BP figures for 2008 indicated a rise in Chinese consumption by 15.8%, representing the largest growth in gas consumption of any country.

This increase in Asia is part of a global pattern of increasing natural gas consumption – estimates are that world demand will increase from 104 trillion cubic feet in 2006 to around 150 trillion cubic feet by 2030.[7] Part of this predicted increase can be attributed to the expectation that natural gas will replace oil wherever possible. Natural gas is therefore a key future energy source for the industrial sector and for electricity generation.

Demand: key points

➤ Consumption is concentrated in North America, Russia, the Middle East and Europe.

➤ Although they are still relatively small markets, Chinese and Indian demand for natural gas is rising quickly.

➤ Demand around the world is expected to increase in the next decade because natural gas is environmentally friendly relative to other fuels.

Supply of natural gas

Given that demand for natural gas is expected to increase, this could put pressure on supply – the Energy Information Administration (EIA) in the United States has suggested that natural gas production will have to increase by between 1% and 2% a year until 2030 to meet demand expansion – but indications are that producers will be able to achieve this. There appear to be sufficient resources of gas to prevent a shortfall of supply to producers in the short to medium term and production totals have been good in the last decade. Indeed, proven natural gas reserves, unlike those of many other commodities, are regarded as plentiful, although their high concentration in the Middle East and Russia means that there would be a significant limitation of supply if extraction in these areas decreased.

Although the supply picture is generally positive, one factor which could influence this is the significant treatment natural gas has to undergo at a

---

[7] Energy Information Administration, International Energy Outlook 2009, www.eia.doe.gov/oiaf/ieo.

processing plant before it can be used as a fuel, which means that there is a maximum production capacity that cannot be exceeded. If demand were to increase more rapidly than expected, this would put pressure on processing capacity.

Supply: key points

➤ Producers will need to increase annual production to meet demand, but they are expected to meet this challenge.

➤ Reserves are plentiful but highly concentrated – with the bulk in the Middle East and Russia.

Natural gas outlook

The fundamentals of natural gas are that reserves are good, but capacity for production is limited and supply is concentrated, which should give support to prices. In addition, if the oil price continues to rise, in theory, so too should the price of natural gas as consumers switch to alternative sources of energy. Concomitantly, if the price of oil comes down, it should be expected that the gas price will follow suit.

In 2009 the price of natural gas was low, which could be attributed to reduced consumption as a result of the global recession – this in turn created a surplus supply. Commentators have suggested that when prices are depressed in this way it is an ideal time to invest in gas funds, and that generally the long-term fundamentals for gas as a result of continued global demand for energy, are strong.

Outlook: key points

➤ The price of natural gas has traditionally moved in tandem with the oil price, as expensive oil increases demand for gas.

➤ In the medium to long term, demand is expected to increase, pushing up the natural gas price.

How To Invest In Energy

Investors wanting to gain exposure to oil and natural gas can invest in ETFs and funds. We will look at both of these below.

ETFs

There are a wide range of energy ETCs available to investors. Some focus on individual resources, such as the ETF Securities **ETFS Crude Oil** or **ETFS Natural Gas**, which track the DJ-UBS Crude Oil Sub-Index[SM] and the DJ-UBS Natural Gas Sub-Index[SM] respectively. There are also ETFs that track heating oil and gasoline.

If you want to invest across the entire energy spectrum and in turn spread your risk, there are basket ETFs available that track various energy indices. For example, investors could opt for the **ETFS Energy DJ-UBSCI[SM] ETC**, which tracks the DJ-UBS Energy Sub-Index[SM]. This product has its allocation spread across crude oil, natural gas, unleaded gasoline and heating oil. As is the case with the individual ETFs, there are also short, leveraged and forward versions of this basket available.

A comprehensive list of energy ETFs can be found in the appendix.

Funds

It is worth pointing out that many mainstream funds (like Invesco Perpetual Income and Fidelity Special Situations) invest in the energy sector and have some exposure to energy stocks, so you don't have to buy a commodity fund to invest in the sector. However, there are a large number of funds that are set up specifically to offer exposure to the energy sector.

One particular fund, that is unusual in that it has direct exposure to energy commodities, albeit with a small exposure to equities as well, is the Alternative Solutions Commodity fund, offered by Schroders and launched in October 2005. It provides exposure to Brent Crude oil, WTI Crude oil and natural gas, as well as having exposure to gold and copper.

Here is a selection of other funds on offer from well-known fund management houses:

➤ The **BlackRock World Energy** fund typically has substantial investments in the oil and gas sectors, with allocations in the exploration and production arenas too.

➤ **Investec Global Energy** invests in a combination of oil producers, refiners and services companies.

➤ The **First State Global Resources** fund has a significant amount of its assets invested in energy-related stocks. The fund also has assets in gold, other precious metals and base metals.

➤ Another well-known group, **Baring Asset Management**, has its own **Global Resources** fund, which invests in firms involved in the extraction, production and processing of commodity-related stocks. It is a heavy energy play, with money also invested in base metals, agriculture and precious metals.

➤ **BlackRock Commodities Income** investment trust has an annual dividend yield target and, over the long term, also aims to provide its investors with capital growth via investments in mining and energy stocks and for its part has a large exposure to oil. Again, it too has a spread across other commodities.

Expert tip

Mark Dampier, head of investment research at Bristol-based financial adviser Hargreaves Lansdown, recommends the **Junior Oils Trust** for more adventurous investors – though of course there is associated risk.

The fund is managed by Angelos Damaskos and invests in relatively small but profitable oil-related companies he believes have the potential to grow rapidly or be targets for a takeover by one of the multinational oil producers.

The top ten holdings in the fund are historically not typical household names, but include/have included Det Norske, Dragon Oil, Soco International, Cirrus Energy and Tullow Oil. Damaskos focuses the fund on his best ideas, holding a concentrated portfolio of around 20 stocks, of which the largest ten typically account for a generous portion. He also keeps a little cash aside to take advantage of any new share issues that come to the market. In the five years since its launch in 2004 the fund has returned more than 100%.

PRECIOUS METALS B

Introduction

Precious metals are rare, naturally occuring elements with a high economic value. In the past they have been used as currency, but in the late 20th and early 21st centuries they have become increasingly regarded as industrial commodities and as stores of value. We will look at the demand and supply considerations, and investing options, for four precious metals: gold, platinum, palladium and silver.

Gold is sometimes referred to as the grandfather of commodities because it is one of the oldest asset classes – the first gold coins were struck by King Croesus of Lydia in 6th century BC. The 'yellow metal', as gold is also known, is soft, malleable and extremely inert. Its near indestructibility means that all the gold that has ever been mined still exists in some form, but this does not make it less valuable.

From the point of view of investors, gold is an enticing proposition. It is highly liquid and unlike cash it is not subject to the credit risk of banks. In addition, when stock markets experience volatility gold is viewed as the asset to turn to because of its low correlation with other investment classes. In other words, gold does not typically follow the ups and downs of shares, property, fixed interest investments (bonds) or cash, and it is also a good hedge against the US dollar. Evidence of this was seen in 2007-08 when the global stock markets were experiencing high volatility. During these uncertain times gold was regarded as a safe haven for investors.

Graham Birch, former manager of **BlackRock Gold & General** fund, has said:

> The recent highs in the gold price are supported by strong demand from investors fearful of the current banking climate. Furthermore, gold has a long history of providing a hedge against inflation, the weak US dollar and geopolitical tension.

Price performance

The performance of gold in between 1999 and 2009 added to its reputation as a stable investment asset. Between January 2000 and December 2009 gold's price increased by 290%, from $283 to $1105 per troy ounce, and throughout the period it experienced arguably relatively low volatility.

Figure 8: gold price (1999-2009)

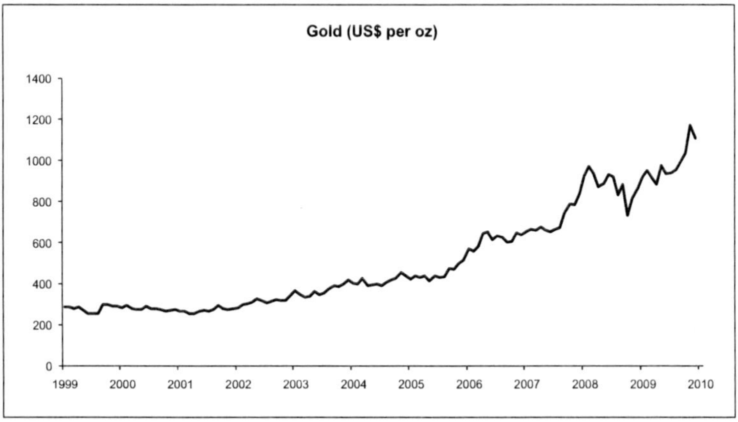

Source: IMF

When compared to the performance of the FTSE 100, gold would have been a good asset for UK investors in the last decade. In particular, as the 2007-09 financial crisis developed, the gold price increased by 44% (between June 2007 and June 2009) as the FTSE slipped by 36%. This strong performance illustrates the yellow metal's tendency to be a good investment prospect during periods of economic instability and stock market uncertainty.

Figure 9: gold price (in sterling) v FTSE 100 Index, rebased to 100 (1999-2009)

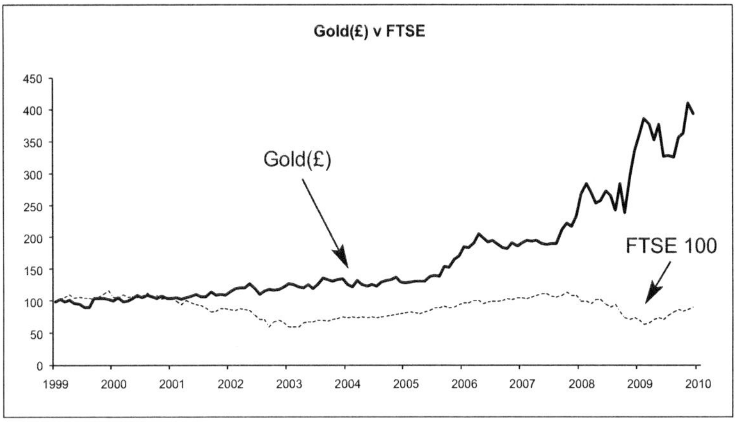

Source: IMF

London gold fixing

Twice each day, at 10h30 and 15h00, the five members of The London Gold Market Fixing Ltd hold a tele-conference to decide the gold price to be used for settling contracts on the London bullion market. The price they decide upon is used as a guideline around the world, although it is not stuck to rigidly and the gold price can begin to move on world markets immediately after it has been fixed in London.

Demand

The three main areas of demand for gold are:

> jewellery,

> industrial use, and

> investment.

Jewellery is said to comprise 70% of all demand for gold. Part of this demand is generated by people buying expensive jewellery as a decorative item, but gold jewellery is also bought as an investment. This suggests that demand for products made of gold is not necessarily tied to the commodity's price – buyers may still purchase items made of gold if they think these represent a stable investment, even if gold is expensive.

Industrial demand for gold is more likely to be affected by its price relative to other commodities that can fulfil the same function and upon broader economic conditions. For example, if gold becomes expensive demand from industry may drop as alternative materials are sought to replace it. Also, in times of recession, as industry is pared back, use of gold in industrial applications can be expected to decrease.

Perhaps the most important consideration for the gold investor is the yellow metal's position as a *hedge against other assets* and as a safe haven during economic disruption. Gold should be expected to be at peak demand during times of recession and stock market volatility because it is regarded as being good at holding its value at these times. Further, when the US dollar is weak – as it generally is during times of global economic disruption – gold is attractive to investors outside the United States due to it being priced in US dollars. The introduction of gold ETFs has boosted demand from the investment side, and this was partly responsible for the strength of gold prices in the last decade.

" Gold should be expected to be at peak demand during times of recession and stock market volatility. "

A final consideration is to think in terms of gold's position as a *store of value*. In view of this, robust demand can be expected from emerging market central banks including those of Russia, South Africa and Argentina. China is also looking to diversify its foreign currency reserves away from the weakening dollar, with gold a consideration. A small increase in China's percentage of gold reserves would cause a rise in demand.

Demand: key points

➤ The largest demand, at around 70% of the total, comes from the jewellery market.

➤ Demand will be at its greatest when stock markets are volatile and economies are weak.

Supply

There are three main areas of supply:

1. it can be mined,

2. central banks can sell off their reserves, and

3. existing gold products can be recycled or resold.

Indications are that gold mines have been producing less gold in recent years. Reserves are not low – there is still a lot of gold in the ground – but it takes time and money to extract it. Falling production rates are caused by a lack of new mines being opened and decreased output from existing mines, both of which can be attributed to reduced investment as a result of the low gold prices in the 1990s. It will take time for the higher gold prices seen since 2000 to translate into increased production, as new mines can take ten years to build and become operational. One example is provided by South Africa, which was the main supplier of gold for much of the last century, but production has fallen in the last decade.

The supply from central banks also looks to be slipping. In the 1980s and 1990s the trend was for central banks to sell their reserves and they flooded the market, depressing gold prices. Now this trend has reversed, and, as mentioned in the demand section, central banks of emerging economies are looking to increase their gold reserves. This points to a falling supply.

Supply: key points

➤ New mine supply is stagnating or falling; South Africa is at 80-year lows. It will take time for new mines to open and for production to be increased.

➤ The balance (one-third) has recently been met from central bank sales and recycling, and this could mean supply is limited.

Outlook

Gold has a worldwide appeal and demand looks as if it will continue to outstrip supply, which suggests that the price will remain strong into the future. Some experts would argue that given these fundamentals gold does not look too expensive at the December 2009 price of $1100 per troy ounce.

Of course, it should be remembered that the price of gold, like that of all commodities, is not immune to volatility. For example, after setting record prices in January 1980, gold plummeted by almost 50% three months later. Prices can and do fluctuate then, but over the long term the price of gold has increased.

Charlie Morris, a fund manager at HSBC Global Asset Management, is a supporter of gold, primarily because of its stability in comparison to other commodities. He said:

> If current trends continue, which I believe they will, gold could reach $2000 per ounce by the year 2014. If you look at gold against other commodities it gives the best risk adjusted returns.

Outlook: key points

➤ Gold is viewed as the ultimate hedge against inflation and any US dollar weakness will push up the price.

➤ Investors flock to gold when there are fears over recession, inflation concerns and geopolitical tensions.

➤ It has been argued that gold is still cheap at the December 2009 price of $1100 per troy ounce.

PLATINUM | 4

The word platinum is derived from the Spanish word *platina*, meaning little silver. Along with palladium, rhodium, ruthenium, iridium and osmium, platinum forms a group of elements referred to as the platinum group metals (PGMs). It is highly valuable because it is extremely rare and its production is time-consuming and costly.

As well as being hard to produce, platinum has unique chemical and physical characteristics meaning that apart from its use in jewellery it is put to a number of industrial and environmental applications. Platinum's uses include LCD displays, spectacles, paint, hard disk drives, fibre-optic cables,

> **" Platinum is highly valuable because it is extremely rare and its production is time-consuming and costly. "**

fertilisers and – perhaps most significantly – catalytic converters, which are fitted to automobiles to reduce toxic emissions such as hydrocarbons and carbon monoxide. In addition platinum-based drugs have been developed to treat a wide range of cancers as the metal is ideal for tiny biomedical components by virtue of its inertness and good electrical conductivity. It is also used in dentistry.

Performance

An analysis of platinum price charts will serve to illuminate some of the considerations that platinum investors need to bear in mind.

Looking at Figure 10, the most obvious incident in the ten-year performance of platinum is the spike in its price in early 2008 and subsequent sharp drop in the second half of the year. The rapid increase in the price at the end of 2007 and early 2008 was caused by disruption to supply in South Africa, where there was a reduction in electrical power reaching mines, meaning that they could not operate at full capacity. This was compounded by investors in platinum ETFs, who helped to push up prices.

Figure 10: platinum price (1999-2009)

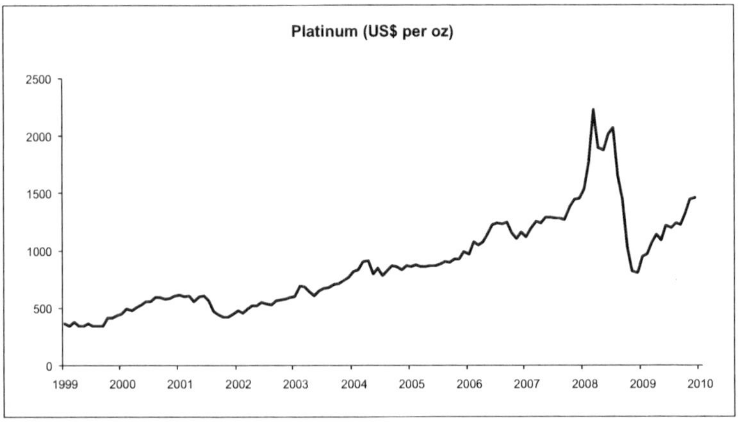

Platinum (US$ per oz)

Source: IMF

The slump of the platinum price – it fell 20% between July and August 2008 alone – was caused by concern over the declining production in the North American automobile industry and ETF investors selling out of long positions.[8]

Despite the volatility of the 2007-2009 period, an investment in platinum would have performed better than an investment in the FTSE 100 in the last ten years. In this period the platinum price increased by 228%. In the last five years the platinum price increased by 70%.

Figure 11: platinum price (in sterling) v FTSE 100 Index, rebased to 100 (1999-2009)

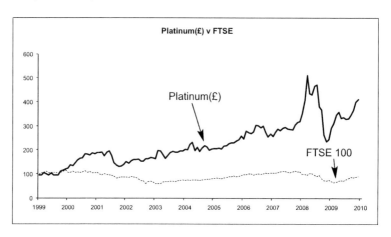

Source: IMF

8 www.platinum.matthey.com/pgm-prices/monthly-price-reports

Demand

Demand for platinum is heavily dependent on automobile manufacturers and the jewellery market, as between them these areas make up 75% of demand for the metal.

In 2009 demand from the automobile sector fell by 33% on the previous year, which can be attributed to reduced vehicle production during the recession. However, the long-term demand should increase. With growing concern about the influence of vehicle emissions on global warming, and with the introduction of legislation in Europe and the United States to combat this, a higher proportion of engines will be fitted with emission-reducing catalytic converters and this will boost platinum demand. It is also worth considering the rising price of oil – as this fuel becomes more expensive diesel vehicles become more attractive and these require higher platinum loadings than petrol engines.

Looking at the other main area of demand, purchases of platinum for jewellery can be elastic, rising or falling depending on how expensive the metal is. In general though, demand should be strong in the medium to long term as world economies stabilise and consumer spending increases.

A final consideration is the proposed introduction of a new platinum-backed ETF in the United States, which is expected in 2010. It is estimated by specialist chemical company Johnson Matthey that this could expand demand by 200,000oz in 2010. To put this in perspective the platinum market was in surplus by approximately 140,000oz in 2009, so an expansion of demand of this magnitude will put pressure on supplies.[9]

Demand: key points

➤ Increased demand is expected from automobile manufacturers as emissions-cutting standards become more strict and economies move out of recession.

---

[9] Miningmx, 'Platinum deficit forecast for 2010',
www.miningmx.com/news/platinum_group_metals/Platinum-deficit-forecast-for-2010.htm

➤ Jewellery demand fluctuates as prices rise and fall.

➤ The introduction of a platinum-backed ETF in the United States could increase demand.

Supply

The majority of platinum – around 75% – is mined in South Africa, which means production conditions there are the most important consideration when thinking about supply. Since the start of the 21st century the situation has not been stable with the result that production levels declined for three years between 2006 and 2008, and remained flat in 2009.

Mining in South Africa is hampered by a number of problems. As more platinum is mined, the mines themselves reach deeper underground, meaning that the extraction of platinum becomes more time-consuming, more costly and less safe. Rather than increase investment to alleviate these issues, some firms have closed mines and others have cut back expenditure. The supply of electricity to mines could also pose difficulties because the South African government's action plan includes a 10% reduction in electricity supply to industrial consumers until at least 2012.

Although the price of platinum increased steadily between 2004 and 2008, which might suggest investment by producers could be expanded and new mines opened, it takes five to seven years for a new platinum mine to begin production and so an immediate augmentation of supply should not be expected.

Supply: key point

➤ Mine production is concentrated in South Africa where expansion programmes are hampered by mine closures, health and safety issues, power shortages and long lead times before new mines begin producing.

Outlook

The bottom line for platinum is that as the world economic situation improves, automobile production levels are anticipated to increase and demand is likely to grow given the necessity of the metal in catalytic converters. This situation is coupled with unstable supplies from South Africa. Taking these factors into account, Bank of America Merrill Lynch forecasted average platinum prices of $1350 an ounce for 2010. This is significantly below the record highs of 2008, but represents an improvement on 2009.

The experiences of oil and gold provide an indication as to what increased speculation from investors will do to the platinum price. Although the introduction of new ETFs will increase demand, perhaps pushing the commodity into a deficit, it is worth remembering that speculative interest can create price volatility.

Outlook: key points

➤ Serious demand in the auto-sector and rising car sales in emerging economies is expected to keep demand momentum up, while supplies from South Africa are unstable.

➤ Increased investor involvement in the platinum market could make the market more volatile.

PALLADIUM | 5

Palladium is a malleable, silvery-white metal with a low melting point and low density. As one of the platinum group metals (PGMs) it has properties in common with platinum, which means it can be put to the same wide range of industrial uses. Palladium is not as precious as platinum because it can also be produced as a by-product of nickel mining.

So numerous is the range of applications for these PGMs that around 25% of all goods either contain them or have had them play a part in their manufacture. One of the major uses of palladium is jewellery, as with all precious metals. In palladium's case, it is cheaper than gold and platinum for manufacturers and customers, so it represents an attractive alternative.

Performance

Palladium has not been the most stable of performers in the last decade. In the last ten years its price dropped by 13%, from $454 to $393 per ounce. In the last five years the price performance was better, representing an increase of 114% from $184 to $393 per ounce.

The relationship between palladium and other precious metals, particularly platinum, becomes evident on looking at Figure 12. As platinum soared to record highs in 2008 (Figure 10) the price of palladium also appreciated as it experienced increased demand as a cheaper alternative.

The most dramatic price movement visible in Figure 12 occurred in late 2000 and early 2001, when the price of palladium surged to above $1000 an ounce. This can be attributed to concern about supply from Russia which arose as the government there were alleged to be considering suspending the sale of palladium from their stockpiles.

Figure 12: palladium price (1999-2009)

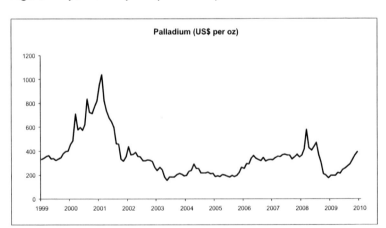

Source: IMF

The comparative chart of the sterling price of palladium and the FTSE 100 (Figure 13) shows that a position in palladium held over the last decade would have only marginally outperformed a position in the FTSE – in December 2009 the palladium price was up 20% on its January 1999 level, while the FTSE was at 90% of the price level at which it began the period.

At its peak in February 2001 palladium was up 130% on its January 2000 price, but by July 2002 the price had sunk back to where it began at the start of the decade.

Figure 13: palladium price (in sterling) v FTSE 100 Index, rebased to 100 (1999-2009)

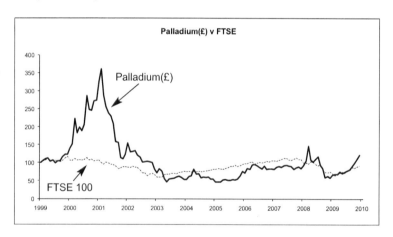

Source: IMF

Demand

The major source of demand for palladium – around 50% – is the automobile industry because like its sister metal platinum it is used in catalytic converters. This means that the considerations for the demand of platinum apply for palladium too – including automobile production in the United States and China, and legislation on harmful emissions from vehicles. While demand has not been at its strongest in the period 2007-2009, it is expected to be high in the next decade as economic conditions improve and industry in China and India advances still further.

Though there is a further wide range of industrial applications for palladium, the second most important sector it is used within is jewellery – making up around 15-20% of demand. Palladium has become increasingly popular as an alternative to platinum in China, Europe and North America because it has a similar appearance and is cheaper.

A third area of palladium demand is investors and ETFs. As with platinum, increased investor participation in the market through new investment vehicles increases demand.

Demand: key points

➤ Demand from the auto-catalyst sector will be strong when vehicle sales are high. Emerging economies, where car-ownership is increasing, are especially important.

➤ There is also demand from industry – palladium is used in computers, mobile phones and televisions – as well as a growing call from the jewellery market.

Supply

The primary sources of palladium are Russia and South Africa. In Russia palladium is a by-product of nickel mining and in South Africa it is a by-product of platinum mining, which can mean that production levels are reliant upon production of these other metals. In particular, the gold and platinum mining problems in South Africa apply equally to palladium.

An issue present in palladium supply for a number of years is the size of Russian stockpiles. During the Cold War the Soviet government stored an unknown quantity of the metal and this has kept the price of palladium low because there has not been a sustained threat of demand vastly exceeding supply since this time. However, it has been suggested that these Russian stocks are now nearing depletion and if this is the case this would have a marked effect on perception about supplies.

Supply: key points

➤ Mining is concentrated in Russia and South Africa. Therefore, the domestic situation in these countries and issues within the mining industries there should be monitored.

➤ Uncertainty surrounds the size of remaining Russian state stocks but these surpluses will not last indefinitely.

Outlook

The fundamentals suggest a good future price performance. Catalytic converter and jewellery demand for palladium is expected to increase, and supplies are concentrated in Russia and South Africa.

Of course palladium is inextricably linked to the other precious metals – a strong performance from gold and especially platinum will see prices for palladium rise as it will become more sought after, but equally a sell off in other precious metals can mean an accompanying depreciation in the palladium price.

Outlook: key points

➤ It is a cheaper substitute for platinum and its fortunes will be tied to the other PGMs.

➤ Conditions in Russia are very important – if stocks there are low and suppliers can only draw on new production this will push prices up.

SILVER | 6

Silver is the least valuable of the four precious metals we focus on, but it has a wide range of important uses due to it being very malleable and its property as the most effective electrical conductor of all metals. Aside from being used to make ornaments, jewellery, coins and of course silverware, it is also used in electrical contacts and conductors, mirrors, photographic film and dentistry. New applications for silver are continuously being explored such as use in batteries, superconductors and microcircuits.

Silver has often been regarded as a cheaper version of gold because it can act as a hedge against other investments and is thought to be a store of value in a similar way to that in which gold is, but at a fraction of the price. This idea does have some merit in that silver's fortunes are customarily tied to those of gold during periods of economic downturn.

> " Silver is mined alongside base metals and so its performance is affected by fluctuations in their prices and production levels. "

However, to say silver merely mirrors gold does not provide the full picture because silver can to an extent be regarded as an industrial metal. Its price is much more dependent on demand from industry than gold's price is. In addition, because silver is mined alongside base metals, fluctuations in the prices and production of these – in particular copper – affect its performance.

Performance

Over the last decade silver displayed a strong performance – rising from $5 per ounce in January 2000 to nearly $17 per ounce in December 2009, an increase of 184%. The five-year performance was also strong – an increase of 227%. However, in late 2009 silver was trading at 84% of its peak price level in this period – the metal had reached as high as $20 an ounce in March 2008.

Figure 14: silver price (1999-2009)

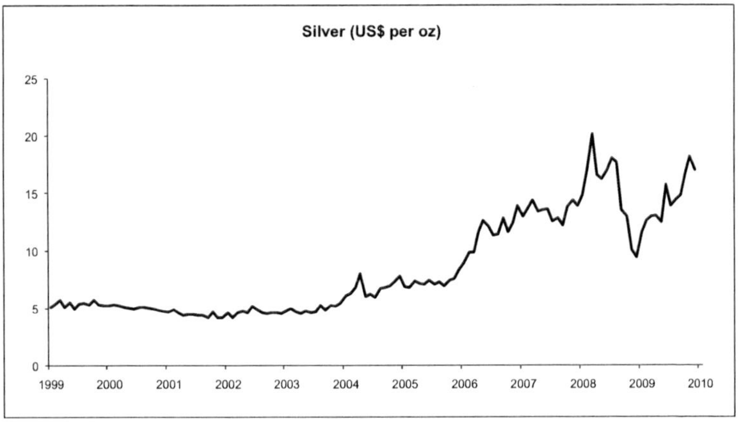

Source: IMF

As you can see from Figure 15, an investment in silver would have outperformed the FTSE 100 over the last ten years as a whole, despite silver showing greater volatility. There is an indication of the inverse correlation between the stock markets and the price of silver provided by the price movement in this period. As the FTSE 100 fell 36% between June 2007 and June 2009, the price of silver was much more stable, increasing by 16%.

Figure 15: silver price (in sterling) v FTSE 100 Index, rebased to 100 (1999-2009)

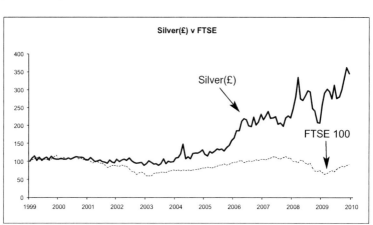

Source: IMF

Demand

The majority of silver demand comes from three sources: industrial uses, jewellery and silverware, and photography. Of these, the industrial uses make up around 50% of total demand. Between 2001 and 2008 even though demand from photography and silverware decreased, increased demand from industry and for coins and medals caused an overall expansion of demand.[10]

The requirements of industry, then, are largely responsible for the increase in silver demand every year between 2001 and the onset of the financial crisis in 2007 and 2008. Even in 2008, at the height of the crisis, demand only dropped by around 1.5%. It is expected that this trend of growth in demand will resume as economies pick up again.

Further demand should be created in the next decade by the growing use of silver in silver-zinc batteries – which are used in electric automobiles.

---

[10] www.silverinstitute.org/supply_demand.php

The Chinese motor vehicle industry is particularly important in this area because it is anticipated that China will look to reduce its dependence on foreign oil and reduce its air pollution in line with international guidelines by expanding the proportion of electric cars it produces. Estimates are that by 2020 half of the automobiles produced in China could be electrically powered.

A final area which creates demand for silver is its use as a hedge against other investments. As speculative interest in silver increases and ETFs – such as the iShares Silver Trust – become more popular with investors supplementary demand will be generated.

Demand: key points

➤ Replenishing of industrial inventories and the production of electric automobiles are areas to watch.

➤ Like gold, silver can be used as a hedge against other assets in times of economic instability. Its importance in industry means that it is also in high demand when economies improve.

Supply

The majority of silver is mined in South America, China and Australia. The levels of supply are contingent upon copper, lead and zinc mining because around two-thirds of silver is mined as a by-product of these metals. This means that the demand for base metals and investment in mining for them can have more of an effect on silver production than an increase or decrease in silver's own price. This situation is described as inelastic – silver supply cannot be increased easily in response to an increase in silver prices.

The Silver Institute reported that in 2008 mine production increased by 3%, but significantly outputs from primary silver mines decreased, as did supply from above-ground stocks such as those held by governments.[11]

---

[11] www.silverinstitute.org/supply_demand.php

This suggests silver is becoming even more reliant on being mined as a by-product of other metals and this will make if difficult for supply to be increased should a need arise.

Supply: key points

➤ Silver supply is inelastic as it is mined as a by-product of base metals.

➤ Another major source of silver – above-ground stocks – will eventually be fully depleted, meaning that mines will be exclusively relied upon for supply.

Outlook

An analysis of silver's fundamentals needs to take account of its duality as both a precious and industrial metal.

Those who see silver primarily as a precious metal point out that it will continue to mirror the performance of gold and thus they present a bearish view of silver's prospects, suggesting that it could slip back into single digits in the short term. The reasoning for this is that when the US dollar strengthens it will reduce silver's characteristic as an investment hedge and push investors away from gold and silver positions, lowering their prices.

Taking a more positive view, those who regard silver as an industrial metal present a picture of price appreciation in the medium to long term. Demand from this area was pushed back between 2007 and 2009, but a recovery in the manufacture and sale of electronic goods will boost demand. The supply side is not weak but it is unpredictable and tied to the fortunes of other metals, which means any sharp increase in demand may not be easy to meet and prices will rise.

On balance, it is customary for silver to be more volatile than gold and investors should be wary of this fact. Therefore, although gold can provide a reference for silver, the performance of industrial metals – in particular copper – should also be taken into account.

Outlook: key points

➤ Silver should be considered both as a precious metal and an industrial metal.

➤ It has traditionally followed the price of gold but it will be susceptible to demand from industry and its supply will be tied to the mining of industrial metals.

How To Invest In Precious Metals

Investors wanting to invest in precious metals have three main options:

1. Direct physical holding of a metal, or having it held elsewhere for you by purchasing a certificate

2. ETFs that track the performance of precious metals

3. Funds

Physical holdings

Perhaps the most obvious way to gain exposure to a precious metal commodity is to buy physical stock of it. With all four precious metals we have covered this can be very simply achieved by purchasing jewellery. Slightly more adventurous is to visit a broker and buy coins. These include the British Sovereign, which has the advantage of being exempt from Capital Gains Tax in the UK. Other popular options are South African krugerrands, the Canadian Maple Leaf and the American Eagle. Gold and silver bullion bars are also an option.

In January 2010, you would have expected to pay around £23,000 for a kilogramme bar of gold. A krugerrand, weighing an ounce, was priced at approximately £750 and sovereigns, which weigh just under eight grammes, were priced at around £200.

For those investors who might find storing physical metal coins or bars impractical – and for insurance purposes it can be – then there is an option to buy certificates from brokers. The metal is then stored on the certificate-holder's behalf, for a fee.

When investing in physical metals it is important to only do business with a reputable dealer. Check the World Gold Council's 'Where To Buy Gold Directory', which can be found on its website[12] and the London Bullion Market Association members list.[13] Both list reputable gold dealers.

ETFs

Precious metal ETFs are very popular with investors because they can offer fast access to an individual precious metal or to a combination of metals. Holdings in exchange traded products physically backed by gold reached $55bn in 2009, which makes them one of the biggest holders of physical gold in the world.

The first option for investors in this area are ETFs that track the spot price of individual precious metals. These include:

➢ **ETF Securities (ETFS) Physical Gold**

➢ **ETFS Physical Palladium**

➢ **Gold Bullion Securities ETC**

There are also ETFs that track indices for each of the precious metals covered here. These include:

➢ **ETFS Gold Exchange Traded Commodity (ETC)**, which tracks the DJ-UBS Gold Sub-Index[SM]

➢ **ETFS Platinum ETC**, which tracks the DJ-UBS Platinum Sub-Index[SM]

➢ **ETFS Silver ETC**, which tracks the DJ-UBS Silver Sub-Index[SM]

Basket ETFs that invest across multiple metals include the **ETFS Precious Metals DJ-UBSCI[SM]**, which is designed to track the DJ-UBS Precious

---

[12] www.invest.gold.org/sites/en/where_to_invest/directory

[13] www.lbma.org.uk

Metals Sub-Index^SM. It invests in gold and silver, with the vast majority allocated to gold.

A comprehensive list of precious metal ETFs can be found in the appendix.

Funds

There are a number of funds available in the UK that offer access to precious metals, although more often than not gold is their primary focus with a smattering of exposure to other precious metals such as platinum or silver. Some can have up to a third invested in other precious metal related stocks.

➤ Arguably the most popular precious metals fund in the UK is the **BlackRock Gold & General** fund, (formerly known as Merrill Lynch Gold & General). The vast majority of the fund is invested in gold-related businesses. The rest is spread typically across platinum, silver and diamonds. At the time of writing, top holdings included Newcrest Mining, Barrick Gold, Lihir Gold and Kinross Gold.

➤ The **J.P. Morgan Natural Resources** fund is an open-ended fund that offers access to gold, although it has exposure to other commodities too, through investments in base metals, agricultural and energy stocks. Two of its largest holdings, again at the time of writing, are Kinross Gold and Lihir Gold – like the **BlackRock Gold & General** fund it also has investments in Barrick Gold.

➤ The Hargearves Lansdown **Junior Mining** fund's main focus is on gold mining shares but it can also invest around 10% in other precious metals like silver, platinum and palladium which have important industrial uses, and 10% in base metal shares like copper and iron-ore. It was launched in 2009.

➤ The **BlackRock World Mining** investment trust has assets invested in the gold sector as well as in platinum, silver, diamond and base metals.

➤ The **BlackRock Commodities Income** investment trust has investments spread across gold, with money in platinum firms too, and assets invested in integrated oil as well as exploration and production-related stocks.

➤ The **Ruffer Baker Steel Gold**, **Investec Global Gold** and the **First State Global Resources** fund are also available to UK investors, and typically have gold exposure.

It is important to remember that funds are a way of diversifying investments and, as such, many funds that invest in precious metals are likely to invest in other commodities such as base metals and energy stocks too.

Expert tip

Mick Gilligan, director of fund research at advisor and stockbroker Killik & Co, likes the **BlackRock Gold & General** fund.

The fund was launched in 1988 and invests mainly in companies involved in the gold mining industry – making it a highly specialised and high-risk investment. On its 20th anniversary in 2008, it celebrated a massive return of 2603%. In other words £1000 invested in the fund when it launched would have been worth approximately £27,000, 20 years on.

The BlackRock team, led by Evy Hambro, aim to invest in gold companies that offer the best exposure to gold prices within an acceptable risk level.

The team follows approximately 500 stocks, including small caps. The portfolio typically holds 40 to 70 companies, the vast majority of which are established gold producers. Gold miners tend to act as a geared play on the gold price.

INDUSTRIAL METALS C

Introduction

Industrial metals, including aluminium, copper, nickel and zinc, are so-called because of the prominent role they have in industry – primarily in construction of buildings, transportation and household products. Copper, nickel and zinc are also known in chemistry as base metals.

The use of these metals in economically-sensitive industries means that they are typically tied to business cycles – when spending on construction, vehicles and new goods by corporations and consumers decreases, so does the demand for industrial metals. In the past this has meant that the condition of the United States' economy, as the largest in the world, was a barometer for industrial metals, but as the economies of China and the other BRIC nations – Brazil, Russia and India – develop this is becoming less so. Spending on infrastructure in the BRIC countries is anticipated to increase in the next decade and as emerging economies grow and prosper, rising incomes, in theory, will support the increased demand for a range of consumer products that utilise these metals.

From a supply perspective, industrial metals tend to be concentrated in just a select few countries and investment, equipment, labour, power supplies and the general infrastructure in these regions are factors that impact the supply of industrial metals.

Their ties to industry and economic growth mean that industrial metals are not like gold and silver in that they do not provide such a strong hedge against stock markets of equities. However, as we will see when comparing the industrial metals to the FTSE 100 index in the following sections, the advantage of these metals is that they offer greater volatility than the FTSE.

This creates opportunities for investors, although it of course creates risks too.

Here we will look further into the background and prospects for aluminium, copper, nickel and zinc, and then outline some ways to invest.

ALUMINIUM 7

Aluminium (or aluminum) has only been commercially produced for around 150 years. Despite its youth, today more aluminium is produced than all other non-ferrous metals combined and it is the most active contract traded on the London Metal Exchange. It is the metal of choice for the automobile, aerospace, rail and marine industries, all of whom make use of its properties as a strong, durable, flexible, corrosion-resistant and lightweight metal. It is also 100% recyclable.

Given these qualities, it is not surprising that aluminium is widely used across a number of industries. In addition to its own properties, when combined with other metals to form alloys it can provide the strength of steel but with just one-third of the weight. This ties its demand somewhat to that for other industrial metals.

Performance

Aluminium has not been a stable performer in the last ten years. The price did increase by 30% in the last decade – from $1680 to $2181 per metric ton – but this does not give the full picture. At its peak in Figure 16 below, aluminium was up 83% on its January 2000 price, trading at $3067 per metric ton in July 2008. It subsequently lost 54% of this price in six months – dropping to $1420 per metric ton in January 2009.

Figure 16: aluminium price (1999-2009)

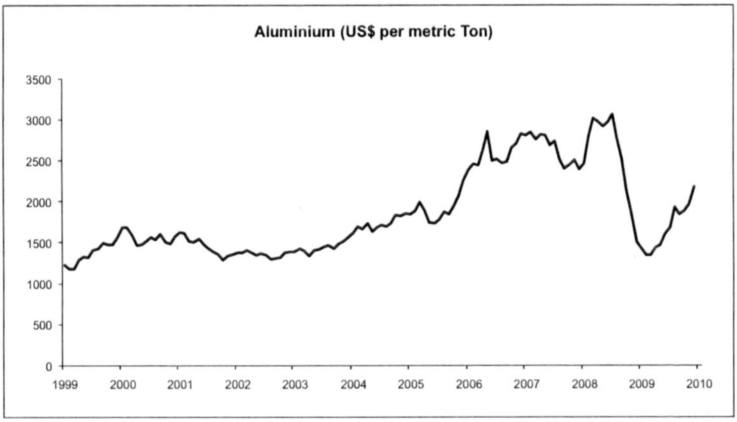

Source: IMF

Even though it has been volatile, the aluminium price outperformed the FTSE 100 index over the last ten years as a whole. Looking at Figure 17 the relationship between the industrial metal and the FTSE becomes evident. When the FTSE dropped 40% between January 2001 and January 2003, aluminium slipped 25%. Similarly, when the aluminium price fell 35% in the six months between July 2008 and January 2009, the FTSE fell 25% in the same period.

Figure 17: aluminium price (in sterling) v FTSE 100 Index, rebased to 100 (1999-2009)

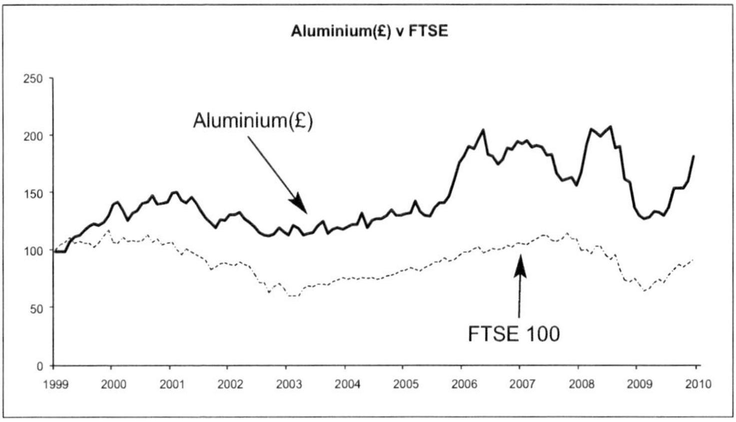

Aluminium(£) v FTSE

Source: IMF

Demand

With its variety of uses, it is of little surprise that aluminium has rapidly become the most-used base metal by tonnage. Its demand is obviously related to how much aluminium is required within the industries in which it is used, and this in turn is dependent upon investment by governments in infrastructure and by private companies in producing new products. In times of economic downturn demand should be expected to fall and conversely in times of economic expansion it will be boosted.

The largest consumers of aluminium are China, the United States, Japan, Germany and Russia, with China alone accounting for 32% of global demand. Even if demand pulls back in the short term, as during the 2007-2009 economic crisis, considering aluminium's uses it is still likely to benefit from the rapid industrialisation and urbanisation of the BRIC countries in the medium to long term.

It is worth thinking about how demand is changing in the countries that use aluminium. In the United States and Japan, approximately 20kg of aluminium is used per capita annually and this level has been steady over recent years. However, in China and India consumption per capita is rising and in theory should one day reach the levels of the United States and Japan. Unless an alternative material with the same properties is found, worldwide demand for aluminium will of course increase.

Demand: key points

➤ China is the world's largest consumer of aluminium.

➤ Rising incomes in industrialising countries should support growing demand for a range of aluminium products in the long term.

➤ Demand is related to wider business conditions – it will vary as sales of consumer goods, for example cars, and investment by construction companies fluctuates.

Supply

The major producing regions for aluminium are China, Russia, North America and Australia, which between them account for more than half of worldwide production. The concentration of production in these areas means that supply is susceptible to disruption, particularly as aluminium production is not always a straightforward process.

A lot of recent production problems have involved electricity; to produce aluminium requires an unhindered supply of electricity, which in turn means that energy makes up a large part of producers' costs. Therefore, power cuts and price rises in energy can mean some smelters have to cut production or close down operations completely. For example, in the United States in 2001, energy shortages sent electricity prices soaring to such an extent that it was more profitable for some aluminium smelters to stop producing the metal and sell their electricity quotas to other users. Conversely, if prices are strong this can enable suppliers to invest in production capacity, by opening closed plants or improving existing facilities, though this process does not occur immediately.

Aluminium does have a different supply dynamic to some other commodities – especially finite commodities such as oil and natural gas – because it is completely recyclable without any adverse effect on its properties. Producing secondary aluminium from scrap is much cheaper than producing primary aluminium, because it requires only 5% of the electricity. This means that access to scrap and output of secondary aluminium are able to balance overall supplies.

Supply: key points

➤ Aluminium production is energy-intensive, thus high energy costs have a large impact on production costs.

➤ Aluminium is able to be fully recycled without any loss of quality.

Outlook

Aluminium was affected by the 2007-2009 financial crisis as demand slipped, lowering prices. However, in the long term there is evidence to suggest prices will be supported.

By far the biggest risk to prices lies with China's appetite for the metal. China dominates the aluminium market in terms of production and demand, which means that any change in that country can make a difference to the global balance and prices. There is nothing to suggest that Chinese economic growth and investment will not continue in the coming years.

The growing industrialisation and urbanisation being carried out in the other emerging economies – where investments are being made in air, roads, rail, transport, packaging, construction, and vehicle usage is anticipated to rise – is also an important factor. It should mean that aluminium experiences a sustained high demand as economies recover and grow once again.

If demand for aluminium rises again in 2010 and beyond, this should see investors buying into it, which will again have a positive effect on the price.

Outlook: key points

➢ China and other industrialising economies dominate the market and so the largest risk to prices lies with their appetites for the metal.

➢ Investors should watch out for news about energy shortfalls affecting production – perhaps caused by hard winters – and investment in smelting plants.

COPPER | 8

Copper is a soft metallic element with a reddish colour. It is a good conductor of heat and electricity. Principle uses include in households as piping and electrical wiring, in electronics, and in construction as a waterproofer. As it is so soft, pure copper can be unsuitable for some of the uses it is put to and so it is regularly combined with other metals to form alloys – brass is an alloy of copper and zinc, and bronze is an alloy of copper and tin. This ties the fortunes of copper to other metals and in fact it has historically been regarded as a bellwether for the base metals markets, meaning that it has been thought the other industrial metals will follow where it leads.

The copper price has been high in recent years, to such an extent that people would steal to get their hands on some. During the decline in the United States' housing market in 2008, reports were

> **“Copper has historically been regarded as a bellwether for the base metals markets. ”**

widespread of thieves visiting vacant properties in search of copper wiring and pipes to sell to scrap metal merchants. In the case of the United States, the average family home uses around 450 pounds of copper. This also suggests that when a housing market is good and new homes and buildings are being constructed demand for copper will be strong. Indeed, as a country's living standards improve, its demand for copper grows and so once again the emerging economies of the world are important considerations.

We will now look at the performance of copper in the last decade and some important supply and demand considerations for the investor.

Performance

As mentioned above, copper was an impressive performer in recent years, although since 2006 it has shown considerable volatility. Between January 2000, when the price of copper per metric ton was $1844, and May 2006, when the price reached $8059, it experienced an increase of 337%. This should be viewed in context though – in 1999 the copper price hit 60-year lows, and part of the subsequent increase was a rebound from this level.

Just as dramatic as the increase between 2000 and 2006 was the plummeting of the price from $8714 per metric ton in April 2008 to $3105 per metric ton in December 2008 – a 65% reduction in eight months. Following this sharp drop copper bounced back once again, making the overall performance for the last decade an increase of 279%.

Figure 18: copper price (1999-2009)

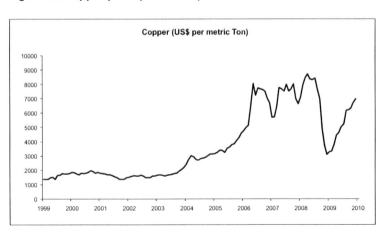

Source: IMF

As can be seen in Figure 19, despite the volatility between 2006 and 2009, copper would have been a rewarding investment in the last ten years, relative to the performance of the FTSE 100. Once again though, it should be considered that copper was at a 60-year low in 1999.

Figure 19: copper price (in sterling) v FTSE 100 Index, rebased to 100 (1999-2009)

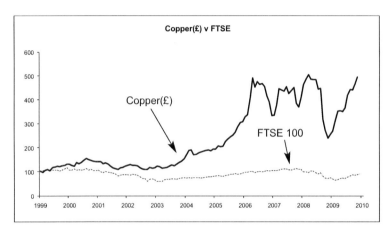

Source: IMF

Demand

Demand for copper follows a similar pattern to the demand for other commodities – when the industries that use it are performing well, copper is sought after and vice versa. Also, demand from emerging economies – with China and India once again foremost among them – cannot be ignored as these countries affect the global balance of the commodity.

China alone accounts for around 25% of global demand, making it the world's largest consumer of copper. It should be anticipated that demand will remain strong into the future – given China's rapidly growing economy and expanding urbanisation – easily rebounding from any dip as a result of the economic downturn between 2007 and 2009.

Meanwhile, consumption in North America, which accounts for 16% of total global demand, fell each year between 2004 and 2008. This could partly be attributed to the financial crisis in 2007 and 2008, but the trend of falling demand was in place before this. Thus it seems, as with aluminium, the important areas to monitor when considering demand for copper are the emerging economies.

Demand: key points

➣ China is the world's largest consumer of copper at around 20%, with demand expected to be robust into the next decade.

➣ As a country's living standards improve, demand for copper grows.

Supply

According to the Copper Development Association (CDA) reserves of copper "are in no danger of running out". Known worldwide resources of the metal are estimated at nearly 5.8 trillion pounds, of which only about 0.7 trillion pounds (12%) have been mined throughout history. The CDA also asserts that nearly all of that 0.7 trillion pounds is still in circulation because copper's recycling rate is high.[14] However, while there is an abundance of large copper deposits, they tend to be in regions of high political risk and extracting some of the reserves is not economically practical. This means a situation of 'peak copper' – the time when the copper extraction reaches its maximum rate – is expected in the next 50 to 60 years.

" There is a concern among producers that prices are being driven by speculators and not by end-users of commodities. "

There are a number of factors to consider. Chile is the world's largest copper producer, making up some 36% of the global supply, but it has been constrained by strikes, power shortages and falling quality. In April 2008

---

[14] www.copperinfo.co.uk

for instance, Chilean state-owned Codelco, the largest copper mining company in the world, faced a number of labour issues as striking subcontractors shut the group's Salvador and Andina mines. Some mining firms are having to dig deeper – only to yield a poorer quality resource – and some of the biggest mines in northern Chile have faced the problem of a decline in natural gas exports from Argentina, meaning they have had to source various alternatives to produce the power they require.

Investment in mines is an important factor in copper supply. There may be plenty of copper left to mine, but if mines are closed due to a lack of investment and existing mines become outdated this will negatively impact supply. Although the copper price has been rising for the past ten years, meaning that investment by producers should be possible, some are reticent to expand production too much because there is a concern that prices are being driven by speculators and not by end-users of copper. Therefore, demand may not be as great as it appears to be. This applies to other commodities too.

Supply: key points

➣ Supplies should not be drastically short as resources of the metal are high and only a small proportion of it has been mined so far. However, it is the mining of the remaining ore that could prove problematic for supply.

➣ Production is concentrated in Chile and has been constrained by strikes, power shortages and falling grades of mined copper.

Outlook

A key factor that could support copper's price is that supply is much more likely to falter than demand. Although economic slowdowns periodically impact upon the demand of copper, its consumption has increased consistently by an average of 4% over the last 100 years and there is no reason to think this long-term trend will change.

Supply, however, is unpredictable and beset with problems. In addition, global refined copper inventories are at about ten days of consumption (meaning that stockpiles are only sufficient to meet ten days' worth of demand), which is close to the all-time lows. Of course, even considering that copper can be recycled, reserves in the ground are finite and so in the long term this supply source will run out.

This does not suggest that copper's price will always rise. It is a volatile commodity and the increased presence of speculators in the market can make price movements less predictable.

Outlook: key points

➤ Annual global copper demand growth is expected to be sustained.

➤ With stocks nearing multi-year lows some analysts believe a concentrated market will not be able to meet demand.

➤ Copper traditionally has been an indicator of where other industrial metals – and silver too – will head.

NICKEL | 9

Nickel is the fifth most common element on earth, after iron, oxygen, silicon and magnesium. It is silvery-white in colour, giving it a similar appearance to silver. Its most important property is its resistance to corrosion, so it is used in plating to protect items made from other materials. Nickel is also used widely in alloys; such as brass and bronze, and in combination with gold and silver. Other uses include coins – which is why the American 5 cent coin carries the moniker "nickel" – and magnets.

Performance

Nickel performed well in the last decade as a whole – it was up 106%, and also increased by 18% over five years. However, as can be seen in Figure 20, nickel was anything but a stable investment. Between May 2006 and May 2007 the price increased by 145% to $51,783 per metric ton, only to then lose 50% of its price by December 2007. By December 2008 there had been a total reduction of 81% in the May 2007 price, as nickel fell to $9847 per metric ton.

Figure 20: nickel price (1999-2009)

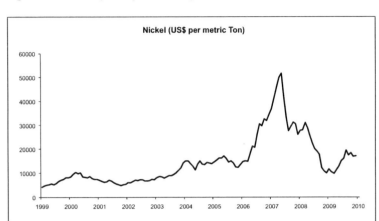

Source: IMF

In spite of its volatility, nickel would have been a better investment in the last ten years than the FTSE 100, if held over the period as a whole. However, as with other commodities, the volatility of nickel means that it is a risky investment. For example, buying into nickel at its height in May 2007, investors would have seen 74% of their investment wiped out by December 2008. By investing in the FTSE at the same time, they would have made a loss of 33% – still a significant reduction, but comparatively not as severe.

Figure 21: nickel price (in sterling) v FTSE 100 Index, rebased to 100 (1999-2009)

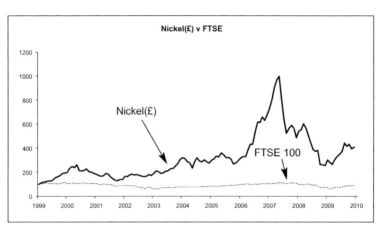

Source: IMF

Demand

As nickel is widely used in industry and building, its demand will be related to economic cycles. In particular, weak demand for stainless steel will create a low demand for nickel because nearly two-thirds of nickel produced is used in stainless steel.

World consumption of nickel increased steadily between 2000 and 2006, at around 4% per year on average, and this pattern could have been expected to continue were it not for the 2007-2009 financial crisis. As it is, the crisis provided a good indication of the disruption to nickel demand when industrial demand slackens. As end users lowered their inventory levels in line with lower output in 2008 and 2009, demand decreased 9% year-on-year and the nickel price dropped markedly.

We have seen with other commodities that demand from China is crucial and nickel is no different. Demand from China increased by 25% each year on average between 2000 and 2009, so that it now comprises around 30% of world demand. Significantly, the demand for stainless steel in

China and India was not weakened as much by the recent financial crisis as was demand from other more developed economies and it showed signs of recovery in 2009.

Demand: key points

➤ China is the largest consumer.

➤ Demand is dependent on economic cycles and in particular demand for stainless steel has an important bearing on nickel consumption.

Supply

The primary mining regions for nickel are Canada, New Caledonia, Australia and Russia. Within the producing regions there are a small number of large smelting and refining operations, which means that supply is susceptible to disruption when one of the large plants lowers output or closes altogether.

With high levels of production in Russia, there has been uncertainty over supply in the past as the producers there are not always open about their production levels and shipping schedules. Other hindrances to supply have included strikes at production plants – such as that at Vale Inco's premises in Canada in 2009.

Supply: key points

➤ Mining operations are spread across twenty countries around the world, but there are a small number of large smelting and refining operations which means supply can be disrupted.

➤ Suppliers have been quick to cut production in times of low demand.

Outlook

There is reason to suspect that nickel will be a stable performer in the short to medium term. With demand dependent on economic growth, it should experience an increase in consumption as world economies recover from recession. In particular, stainless steel requirements in China, India, Brazil and Russia should be a large source of demand for nickel. Stainless steel is an important material in infrastructure development – in terms of transport and architecture – and these countries are expected to continue to invest in these areas.

A repeat of the price bubble – including rapid rise and subsequent collapse – between 2006 and 2009 seems unlikely because if demand and prices increase, suppliers should be able to re-open operations they have previously closed to boost supply. As with any industrial commodity though, an unexpected disruption to supply or sharp drop in inventory levels will attract the interest of speculative investors and push prices up.

Outlook: key points

➤ Demand for stainless steel from the BRICs is expected to be strong in the next decade and beyond.

➤ Volatility is always a possibility as indicated by the past ten years of price activity.

ZINC	**10**

Zinc is a bluish-grey metal found in the earth's crust in the form of ores. Its fortunes are typically tied to those of copper, with which it is combined to make brass; aluminium, with which it is combined to make zinc-aluminium alloy; and steel or iron – which it is used to galvanise. As zinc is more reactive than other industrial metals it is ideal for use in galvanisation as it reacts readily with air. For this reason zinc is put to use to protect cars, bridges and wire fences. Fifty per cent of zinc is used in this way. It is also used in batteries, coins and in medicine.

Performance

Zinc was a good performer in the last ten years, with a 100% price increase from $1179 to $2374 per metric ton. Over the last five years the increase was a little less significant, at 91%. It is clear from viewing Figure 22 that zinc experienced a pattern similar to that of the other industrial metals between 2006 and 2009, increasing rapidly to a peak of $4381 per metric ton in December 2006 before losing 75% of this price level in the following two years and falling as low as $1113 per metric ton in December 2008. Subsequently, the zinc price increased rapidly once again – rising 97% in 2009.

Figure 22: zinc price (1999-2009)

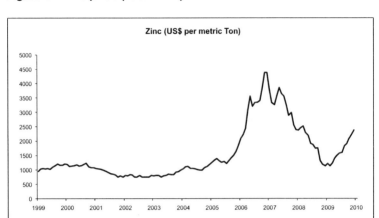

Source: IMF

Neither the zinc sterling price nor the FTSE 100 index performed exceptionally between 1999 and 2005, with zinc marginally the better investment. The performance of zinc from 2006 onwards, even taking into account the price drop in 2007 and 2008, meant that over the decade shown in Figure 23 it was a better investment than the FTSE 100 overall.

Figure 23: zinc price (in sterling) v FTSE 100 Index, rebased to 100 (1999-2009)

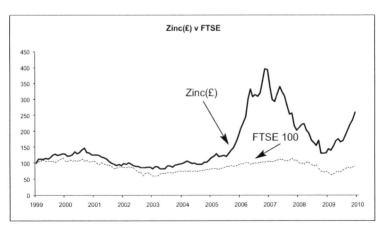

Source: IMF

Demand

With demand for zinc dependent upon the transportation and construction sectors, it is natural that China should be foremost among consumers of the metal as it invests heavily in these areas. Even though demand from the United States and Europe has not been expanding in recent years – particularly since 2007 – demand from China and India is anticipated to grow as new buildings are constructed and car ownership increases.

The United States is another large consumer of zinc but end-use zinc consumption is closely correlated to some of the weakest performing sectors of the United States' economy in recent years and so demand has been relatively weak. The United States' economy is expected to strengthen in the short to medium term though, and this bodes well for zinc demand.

Zinc is inextricably linked to those metals it is used alongside in making alloys and those metals it is used to galvanise. This means if demand for copper, iron and steel is strong – and of course the performance of these metals depends on world economic growth too – then demand for zinc will be strong.

Demand: key points

➤ China is the largest consumer of zinc.

➤ It is used to galvanise metals to prevent corrosion and therefore used extensively in the automobile industry.

Supply

Zinc reserves are reasonably strong. Up to the beginning of the 21st century around 350 megatonnes of zinc had been extracted throughout history, one-third of which is still in use. With around 500 megatonnes of reserves remaining, estimates have suggested supplies from mines will be depleted in the next 25 to 50 years. This means exhaustion of supply is not a consideration for the investor in the short to medium term, particularly as one-third of zinc production is accounted for by recycling old zinc products.

The nature of zinc production is that it is spread widely around the world, with a lack of integration between mining and smelting operations in different countries. This means that in the past producers have been slow to react to poor market conditions. Their incentive for this is partly that closing mines altogether is expensive, and producers hope that their competitors will cut production first, meaning they do not have to. Thus, at times of low demand production is not cut quickly and an over-supply can occur.

Supply: key points

➤ China is the biggest producer – accounting for 30% of world production.

➤ Producers have traditionally been slow to cut supplies in reaction to low prices.

Outlook

The recent history of zinc can provide clues as to what may happen with the metal in the future. As we saw, the zinc price escalated through 2006 to a peak at the end of that year and the beginning of 2007. Producers were encouraged by this to invest in and expand their operations. Then, as demand fell in 2007 prices were pushed lower, forcing producers to scale back.

Since that time prices have not rebounded sufficiently to encourage an expansion of supply and it is likely that when demand does increase it will take some time for supply to be increased to meet this. It is true that there has been restocking of inventories in recent months, with London Metal Exchange reserves up by 93% in the last year, but the overall levels are still low by historic standards.

Overall, although there is not expected to be a drastic shortfall of supplies and a rapid rise in price in the short term, the prospects for zinc appear good as demand improves. Investors should have renewed confidence in all industrial metals, which is good for zinc.

Outlook: key point

➤ Supplies are stable for now, but as demand increases it will take time for production to rise and meet it. This will support prices.

How To Invest In Industrial Metals

The easiest option for investors wanting to gain exposure to industrial metals is ETFs. Funds and investment trusts are also available.

ETFs

ETF Securities have a number of different ETFs that can give investors easy access to the base metals market. They come in long, short or leveraged versions, and include:

➤ **ETF Securities (ETFS) Aluminium Exchange Traded Commodity (ETC)**, which tracks the DJ-UBS Aluminum Sub-Index^{SM}

➤ **ETFS Copper ETC**, which tracks the DJ-UBS Copper Sub-Index^{SM}

➤ **ETFS Nickel ETC**, which tracks the DJ-UBS Nickel Sub-Index^{SM}

➤ **ETFS Zinc ETC**, which tracks the DJ-UBS Zinc Sub-Index^{SM}

Investors wanting to access base metals and spread their risk could opt for a basket ETC, such as the **ETFS Industrial Metals DJ-UBSCI^{SM} ETC**, which tracks collectively the fortunes of copper, aluminium, zinc and nickel on the DJ-UBS Industrial Metals Sub-Index^{SM}.

A comprehensive list of industrial metal ETFs can be found in the appendix.

Funds

There are a variety of portfolios available to investors that access the base metals market:

➤ One of the most popular commodity funds available to UK investors is the **J.P. Morgan Natural Resources** fund – the hugely successful portfolio typically has a substantial amount of investments in base metals related companies, as well as money in other areas, such as energy firms, agricultural commodities and precious metals.

➤ The **Oceanic CF Global Resources** is popular with financial advisors. The Australia-based group invests in the shares of firms involved in the mining, extraction and/or processing of natural resources and associated operations and infrastructure. It will also typically have exposure to base metals, as well as to precious metals and energy-related stocks.

➤ The **First State Global Resources** invests in the shares of companies in the natural resources and energy sectors worldwide. It has assets invested in the metals sector, with other monies invested in energy and precious metals.

➤ The **BlackRock World Mining** investment trust is another strong metals play with assets invested in base metal related stocks – as well as in gold, platinum and diamond investments. Its sister fund, the **BlackRock Commodities Income** investment trust – which has an annual dividend yield target and, over the long term, also aims to provide its investors with capital growth via investments in mining and energy stocks – also has investments in the base metals area, alongside exposure to precious metals, coal, and iron ore.

➤ Other funds that invest in the base metals sector are available from well-known investment houses such as Baring Asset Management, Martin Currie and Schroders.

Expert tip

Darius McDermott, of London-based financial adviser Chelsea Financial Services, recommends **ETFS Industrial Metals DJ-UBSCI^{SM}** for those investors looking to get into the base metals sector. It tracks collectively the fortunes of copper, aluminium, zinc and nickel on the DJ-UBS Base Metals Sub-Index.

McDermott also likes the **J.P. Morgan Natural Resources** fund. Again this is a high-risk play but its performance figures make good reading for its investors – between the end of 1971 and mid-2009, it rose by a spectacular 6687%.

The fund has investments in base metals but also in other commodities including precious metals. It is managed by Ian Henderson, one of the longest-serving fund managers and an acknowledged expert in the commodities field. McDermott says:

> This fund is the definition of a shoot-the-lights-out fund. It's high-risk but offers potentially very high returns.

AGRICULTURE D

Introduction

The agricultural commodities are corn, wheat and soybeans. These are otherwise called the *soft commodities,* or the *grains*, although strictly soybeans are oilseeds rather than grain. These commodities are fundamental in producing food for the world's inhabitants, but also are increasingly used in biofuels. Obvious pressures are the land used for their cultivation, weather and the growing human population. Also important is the price of oil: as this fuel becomes more expensive and less abundant, alternative fuels – including biofuels – will be sought.

These factors, among others, have meant that agricultural commodities have performed strongly in recent years.

Soft commodities producers can react quickly

It is important to consider how quickly producers can react to high prices to increase the quantities of corn, wheat or soybeans they intend to grow in a given season. We noted earlier that gold, palladium and platinum mines can take up to a decade to become operational, which means even with sustained high prices it takes a long time for new supplies of precious metals to emerge. This in turn provides further support for prices. This is not the case with wheat or other soft commodities – farmers can increase the amount of land they give to corn, wheat or soybeans the very next growing season, which means supply can be boosted quickly and prices are pushed down. This suggests that sustained booms over a long period are not likely in agricultural commodities and their prices can show high volatility.

CORN | 11

Also known as maize, corn is a cereal grain widely cultivated around the globe. It is a staple food in many countries, both for humans and for livestock. Corn is also increasingly used as a biofuel, albeit not the same variety as can be eaten by people. In this role, it is used as a feedstock for ethanol, which is then mixed with gasoline to reduce the harmful emissions from automobile engines. This use of corn for fuel purposes has led to a situation where the price of corn tracks the price of oil – if oil is expensive, corn becomes expensive as an alternative fuel source.

Performance

The performance of corn in the last decade was strong, with the price per metric ton increasing from $93 in January 2000 to $165 in December 2009 – an increase of 77%. However, at the end of this period corn was down 43% on its high in June 2008.

The relationship of corn and oil is indicated by Figure 24. In this chart the corn price peaked at around $290 per metric ton in June 2008, which is the same month as oil peaked at around $135 a barrel (Figure 4).

Figure 24: corn price (1999-2009)

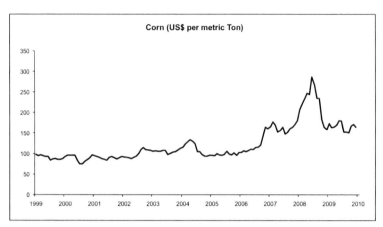

Source: IMF

Looking at where corn started and ended the period 1999-2009, it was a good performer relative to the FTSE in these years, although it did show volatility along the way. To the end of 2006 the FTSE and the sterling corn price were pretty much even performers, but the rapid increase in the corn price in 2007 and 2008 meant it ended this ten-year period as a better performer than the FTSE.

Figure 25: corn price (in sterling) v FTSE 100 Index, rebased to 100 (1999-2009)

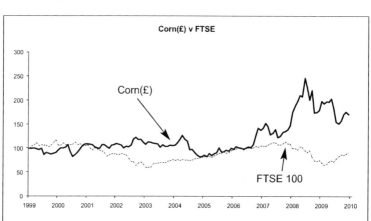

Source: IMF

Demand

Demand for corn can be broken down into three "Fs":

➢ Food – for humans

➢ Feed – for animals

➢ Fuel – for automobiles

The most obvious use of corn is as a food and, unsurprisingly, the country where this demand has been expanding most is China. Chinese consumption of corn has increased every year for the last two decades – growth that has been founded on an enlarging and increasingly affluent population. Not only do the more mouths to feed mean that more corn is needed, but as a proportion of the Chinese population gets richer, they are including more meat and dairy products in their diets, which means more grain is needed to feed livestock.

As mentioned above, corn is used to make ethanol for biofuels and, in particular, demand from the United States has been galvanised by its expanding ethanol industry, which has consistently increased its share of the corn use each year since the mid-1990s. In 2007, during his State of the Union address, then United States President George W. Bush declared that the solution to high energy prices is to find alternative energies. As such, his message was that the government should sharply raise the mandate for ethanol use in motor fuels, setting a floor for alternative and renewable fuel use in 2017 that is equal to seven times the current ethanol output.

> **"** The increasing demand for biofuels in the US is one cause of the rising price of corn. **"**

Ethanol is a 'green' alternative to petrol and the increasing demand for biofuels in the United States – particularly for corn-based biofuels – is one cause of the rising price of corn. However, it should not be automatically assumed that corn-based biofuels will continue to be widely used, because it has been questioned whether corn-based ethanol is really as green as it seems; some research has shown that more energy (provided by fossil fuels) is needed to create ethanol than it can produce.

The use of previously-forested land for the cultivation of corn has also been opposed and of course with the world's population increasing there are questions over whether it is practical to grow 'fuel' on land that could be used to grow food. Even with these qualifications, the EU and United States are committed to reducing harmful emissions and biofuels are regarded as an important method in achieving this.

Demand: key points

➤ Corn is a staple food and this is unlikely to change in the short or medium term – demand will still be strong from this area.

➤ Growing demand from China's large population.

➤ Concerns over emissions from motor vehicles and the rising price of oil mean that corn is in demand to make ethanol for biofuel. This is not a straightforward issue, but for the time being at least, biofuels are regarded as a fuel for the future.

Supply

The United States and China are the two leading producers of corn – between them accounting for around 60% of the world's total – and it is also grown in Africa, Europe and South America. Recent supply reports from the United States Department of Agriculture (USDA) were positive, placing the total supplies in the United States as of September 2009 at 14.5bn bushels – the highest levels on record.

Other considerations on the supply side include political occurrences – such as when Argentina increased export duties on corn by 44% in 2008 – and of course the weather and its impact on harvests.

Supply: key points

➤ Pressure on stocks from rising demand, notably in China.

➤ The United States will divert a larger proportion of its resources to making ethanol.

➤ Poor harvests limit supply and push prices up.

Outlook

It is difficult not to see a strong performance for corn in the future. Each year there are more people and more cattle on the planet that need to be fed, which means demand for food will continue to rise. Demand for alternative fuel sources will also be strong because of concerns about emissions from engines and as oil becomes increasingly scarce **"As long as demand remains strong a bad harvest or other disruptions to supply could cause prices to rise. "** in the medium to long term. Although supply from America does not appear to be weak, as long as demand remains strong a bad harvest or other disruptions to supply could cause prices to rise.

Remember that a link has emerged between the prices of corn and oil – in line with corn's use in producing fuel. The performance of the fossil fuel should be monitored when investing in corn.

Outlook: key points

➤ For the moment supplies are not expected to fall short of demand, but disruption to supply could change this situation.

➤ A link has emerged between the performances of corn and oil.

S O Y B E A N S | 12

Soybeans, or soya beans, are oilseeds native to East Asia, but which are now grown mostly in North and South America. They are an important crop because they have a wide range of uses for food and in industry; soybeans are used in vegetable oil, high-protein meat and dairy substitutes, animal feed – for livestock and pets – and in biodiesel.

Performance

The soybean price was up 110% in the last decade, rising from $180 to $379 per metric ton. The soybean price was also up over the last five years, increasing by 94%. As is evident from looking at Figure 26, however, the soybean price experienced volatility in the past ten years.

Figure 26: soybeans price (1999-2009)

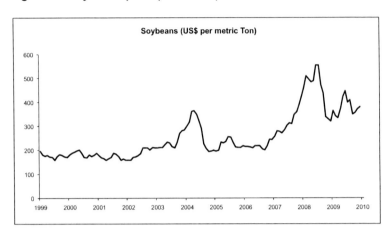

Source: IMF

Soybeans outperformed the FTSE 100 in the last ten years as a whole. As with the other commodities we have looked at so far, soybeans would have represented a good buy-and-hold investment but investing in the short term would have been risky.

Figure 27: soybeans price (in sterling) v FTSE 100 Index, rebased to 100 (1999-2009)

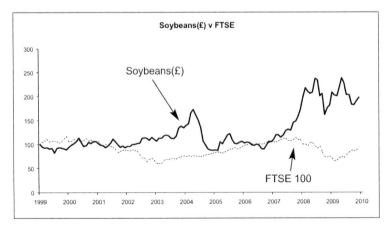

Source: IMF

Demand

The demand for soybeans mirrors that of corn – demand for human food, animal feed and biofuel.

China, as discussed, has been rapidly upping its protein intake – hence a rising demand for corn and soybeans to use in animal food – and it is now the world's largest importer and consumer of soybeans. This means that demand from China is key to world soybean demand.

In the same way that corn is used to make the biofuel ethanol, soybeans are used to create biodiesel – a environmentally friendly version of diesel. An indication of how this use of soybeans can affect prices was provided when surging petroleum prices in 2008 provided strength to soybean oil demand.

As with other commodities, demand for soybeans can be affected by world economic conditions. It should be considered that investment in alternative energies such as biodiesel is impacted by recession and when consumers have less money to spend they may buy fewer expensive meat products, which means less animal feed is needed.

Biodiesel

According to the United Soybean Board (USB), using soy biodiesel significantly reduces the exhaust levels of many greenhouse gases, and it is less toxic than table salt and biodegrades as quickly as sugar. In addition there is much more energy in a gallon of soy biodiesel than is required to produce it. Another benefit attached to growing crops like soybeans is that they take carbon dioxide out of the atmosphere to use for photosynthesis.

Demand: key points

➤ Demand from the United States and China is very important and is likely to be strong from both countries into the future.

➤ If pressure to move from traditional diesel to biodiesel increases this will in turn increase demand for soybeans.

Supply

The top three soybean producing countries are the United States, Brazil and Argentina, together contributing around 80% of world totals of the crop. Within these main growing countries, the major factors that can affect yields and supplies are weather, and thus quality of harvests, and acreage given over to the growing of soybeans.

Growing conditions, including weather, can be unpredictable but acreage and yields are monitored by such groups as the USDA. Investors should keep up-to-speed with their reports when investing in soybeans. The most likely pressure on acreage comes from other agricultural commodities – for example if corn prices are high and more corn is needed for ethanol production this can squeeze the amount of land used for cultivating soybeans.

Another factor that experts discuss is the exports from South America. If these are increased, following strong harvests, this might provide higher supply quantities.

Supply: key point

➤ Acreage, yields and quality of harvests in the United States, Brazil and Argentina are important.

Outlook

The soybean boom of 2007 and 2008 is over but with three notable price spikes in soybean prices since 2004 the indications are that soybeans will continue to be a volatile prospect, with opportunities and risks for investors.

Ultimately soybean market fundamentals remain in a robust state of health, for four primary reasons – strong Chinese demand, strong interest in biodiesel production, changeable global production and competition for United States acreage from other crops, including corn. With demand strong and unlikely to fluctuate widely it is supply that should be most closely observed by investors.

Outlook: key points

➢   Strong supply rather than weak demand is most likely to affect prices.

➢   Overall soybean demand is expected to rise in the long term as the world's population increases.

W H E A T 13

A large number of people in the world eat some kind of food made from wheat every day. It is used to make flour for biscuits, cakes, bread and pasta, and is fermented to make alcohol and biofuel. Wheat is also grown for use as forage for livestock.

In recent years wheat production and its price has been the subject of scrutiny by governments and the UN because of its importance for feeding such a large number of people. Bad harvests – such as those of 2007 caused by freezing weather and flooding in Europe and drought in Australia – can generate panic about supply and this pushes prices up. Any such increase in prices is felt directly by consumers when they buy groceries.

Performance

The wheat price was up 95% in the last ten years, increasing from $106 to $206 per metric ton. As Figure 28 shows however, the price did not rise steadily – it hit nearly $440 per metric ton in March 2008, only to lose 30% of this price level in six months as it fell to $296 per metric ton in September 2008.

This price spike can be partly attributed to the overall boom in agricultural commodities in 2007 and 2008, and partly to the poor wheat harvests of 2007 discussed above.

Figure 28: wheat price (1999-2009)

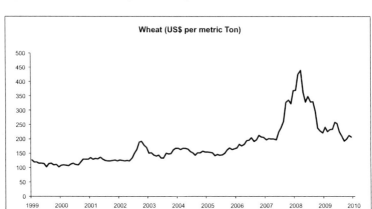

Source: IMF

An investment in wheat would have been good for UK investors in the past ten years, relative to a position in the FTSE 100. Between January 1999 and October 2000 the FTSE slightly outperformed wheat, but from this point until December 2009 wheat was up 61% while the FTSE dropped 16%.

Figure 29: wheat price (in sterling) v FTSE 100 Index, rebased to 100 (1999-2009)

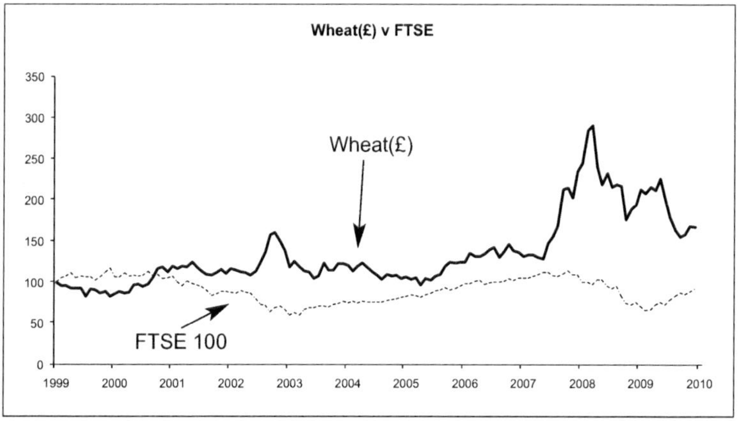

Source: IMF

Demand

As would be expected, countries with large populations provide most of the demand for food and hence for wheat. Foremost in wheat consumption levels is China, followed by India, Russia and the United States. Unlike with some other commodities, consumption of wheat tends to be fairly inelastic – meaning it does not vary much from year to year – and demand has grown by around 1% a year for the past decade.

This does not mean that demand will never fluctuate – as one of the agricultural commodities demand for wheat is related to demand for both corn and soybeans. For instance, if the corn price rises significantly it may become too expensive as a feed for animals and wheat may come into greater demand as an alternative food source.

Demand: key points

➤ Staple crop for a huge portion of the world's population.

➤ Demand for wheat is related to demand for the other soft commodities.

Supply

As with other agricultural commodities, investors should keep up-to-speed with wheat production news from the major growing areas. These include China, India, North America, France and Australia. Good sources for this are the USDA *Wheat Outlook* publication, which is published monthly, and the news on the wheat trade published by the Grains Council of Australia.

In all of the major wheat producing countries, an important supply consideration is the acreage given to wheat seeding. There is competition for land from other commodities – including soybeans and corn – and from cattle farming. Pressure on governments to increase the production of biodiesel can mean that land that might be used for wheat is used to cultivate soybeans.

" Investors in agricultural commodities should keep up to speed on news from the major growing areas: China, India, North America, France and Australia. "

Supplies have been unstable in the recent past, as the rally in wheat prices to an all-time high in 2008 showed. This was primarily attributable to the supply shortfall that emerged in the global wheat market in the wake of adverse climatic conditions – three years of disappointing harvests severely took their toll; exports were limited from some major producing regions in order to control domestic food inflationary concerns and ensure adequate supplies. There is of course potential that this kind of disruption could occur again following bad harvests or as a consequence of a sharp rise in demand.

The price of oil is also important. Diesel is needed to power essential machinery in the production and transportation of wheat, so if oil is expensive this will increase the cost of production and supplies will be affected.

A last point to consider is that wheat-producing countries keep inventories of the commodity and these can help mitigate the effects of bad harvests by augmenting supplies. When growing conditions are favourable – as they were in the United States in 2009 – this allows producers to top-up their stocks.

Supply: key points

➤ Supply is dependent upon suitable weather for growing wheat.

➤ Acreage allocation in the major growing regions is a key supply-side factor for the market.

➤ Production levels of soft commodities can easily be increased to boost supply in response to high prices.

Outlook

Demand for wheat is firm because it goes into producing vital foodstuffs but supplies are not weak and the price is unlikely to escalate rapidly in the short to medium term. However, as was seen in 2007 and 2008, two or three consecutive bad harvests can have a marked effect on the wheat price and this situation could easily recur.

The fermentation of wheat to make biofuels is an important dynamic. If greater proportions of wheat are used in the production of environmentally friendly fuel this leaves less to be used to make food, which will support prices. Pressure on governments to reduce emissions from vehicles will then have to be weighed against protests from consumers against high prices of basic foods.

It is impossible to invest in one of corn, soybeans or wheat in isolation without giving some consideration to the others.

Overall, wheat's place as one of the soft commodities should not be ignored; it is impossible to invest in one of corn, soybeans or wheat in isolation without giving some consideration to the others as each tends to follow where the others lead.

Outlook: key points

➤ Wheat should always be considered within context as one of the agricultural commodities and by looking at trends in other commodities – in particular oil.

➤ An enlarging world population means there is unlikely to be a collapse in demand, meaning a sustained reduction in supply could create a shortfall and high prices.

How To Invest In Agriculture

Investing in agricultural commodities is as easy as it has ever been – as before, we will focus on ETFs.

ETFs

There are ETFs available that track the individual performance of the three agricultural commodities covered here and each of these is available as either a long, short or leveraged investment. These include:

➤ **ETF Securities (ETFS) Corn Exchange Traded Commodity (ETC)**, which tracks the DJ-UBS Corn Sub-Index^{SM}

➤ **ETFS Soybeans ETC**, which tracks the DJ-UBS Soybeans Sub-Index^{SM}

➤ **ETFS Wheat ETC**, which tracks the DJ-UBS Wheat Sub-Index^{SM}

In addition there are basket ETCs available that enable long, short or leveraged investments in wheat, corn and soybeans at the same time. These include the **ETFS Grains DJ-UBSCI^{SM} ETC**, which tracks the DJ-UBS Grains Sub-Index^{SM}.

A comprehensive list of agriculture ETFs can be found in the appendix.

Funds

As mentioned, historically, investors have not had it easy when it came to investing in agriculture. However, such has been the recent demand for agricultural commodities and related investments, a number of new investment vehicles have hit the market.

Such was the popularity of the £3.3bn **Schroders Alternative Solutions Agricultural Commodities** fund that early in 2008 it closed its doors to new investors – just 17 months after it launched. They did this because the fund management group thought they could better serve investors by not getting too big. No doubt as a result of investor demand for access to the agricultural commodity super cycle, the group was quick to launch an agricultural land investment trust. The **Schroders Agricultural Land** fund offers exposure to agricultural land and land-related industries as well as agriculture-related private equity companies, farm management businesses and related funds.

Investors who want access to the group's expertise could go for its sister fund, **Schroders Alternative Solutions Commodity** fund. Launched in October 2005 it provides exposure to agricultural commodities as well as metals and energy.

The **Eclectica Agriculture Fund**, launched in June 2006, invests in companies which are involved in, connected to, and/or related to agriculture and farming issues. Hugh Hendry, co-fund manager, looks to companies manufacturing products such as tractors, fertilisers and crop protection for investment opportunities in the sector.

Others too have responded quickly to the boom in agriculture. Sarasin introduced its **AgriSar** fund and Baring Asset Management brought out its **Agriculture Fund** in 2008. The latter focuses on companies where the majority of earnings come from activities relating to the sector. It will look at everything from agrichemicals producers to seed manufacturers, farming, farm land, grain handlers and even shipping companies where it sees investment opportunities.

In terms of investment trusts, the **Ceres Agriculture** fund from FourWinds Capital Management is an agriculture-focused portfolio, but is unusual in that it invests primarily in ETCs – it is an investment trust that invests in exchange traded commodity funds. More recently, another group, Pictet, launched its own agriculture fund.

Expert tip

Justin Urquhart Stewart of Seven Investment Management recommends the **ETFS Grains**, which is allocated to wheat, corn and soybeans.

He says:

> This is a good starting point for investors looking at agricultural commodities. It is transparent and easy for investors to understand. With an increasingly restricted supply of key commodities such as corn, soybeans and wheat, I am optimistic on agricultural commodities in the long run. The market will see periods of sharp corrections, it will go up and down, but over the long term the story behind investing in agricultural commodities and especially grains is very compelling.

APPENDIX

·

Commodity ETFs Listed On The LSE

The following tables include the commodity-related ETFs listed on the London Stock Exchange in the following categories:

1. Energy

Table 1a: Energy commodities

Table 1b: Leveraged energy commodities

Table 1c: Short energy commodities

Table 2a: Energy indices

Table 2b: Forward energy indices

Table 2c: Leveraged energy indices

Table 2d: Short energy indices

Table 3: Energy-related stock indices

2. Precious metals

Table 4a: Precious metal commodities

Table 4b: Leveraged precious metal commodities

Table 4c: Short precious metal commodities

Table 5a: Precious metal index

Table 5b: Leveraged precious metal index

Table 5c: Short precious metal index

Table 6: Precious metal-related stock indices

3. Industrial metals

Table 7a: Industrial metal commodities

Table 7b: Leveraged industrial metal commodities

Table 7c: Short industrial metal commodities

An explanation of the columns in the tables:

1. *ETF*: The name of the ETF

2. *TIDM*: The LSE code for the ETF.

3. *SEDOL*: A security identifier used in the UK.

4. *ISIN*: An international security identifier.

5. *Country of ETF Registration*: For example, ETF Securities is incorporated in Jersey (JE).

6. *Price Currency*: Most ETCs are priced in US dollars (USD), although some are priced in sterling (GBP). (Note that regardless of the price currency of the ETC, nearly all commodities themselves are priced in US dollars and that is where the currency exposure lies.)

7. *Average Daily Volume*: The number of shares traded daily averaged over a period of 100 days.

8. *Beta*: A measure of the extent to which the ETC rises or falls relative to the FTSE 100. If an ETC has a beta of 1.0, then if the FTSE 100 rises 10% the ETC has historically also risen 10%. If an ETC has a beta of 0.5, then if the FTSE 100 rises 10% the ETC has historically risen 5%. If an ETC has a beta of -0.5, then if the FTSE 100 rises 10% the ETC has historically fallen 5%.

1. Energy

Table 1a: Energy commodities

ETF	TIDM	SEDOL	ISIN	Country of ETF Registration	Price Currency	Average Daily Volume	Beta
ETFS Crude Oil	CRUD	B15KXV3	GB00B15KXV33	JE	USD	231,000	0.9
ETFS Forward Heating Oil	HEAF	B24DM02	JE00B24DM021	JE	USD	33,000	0.8
ETFS Forward Natural Gas	NGAF	B24DM35	JE00B24DM351	JE	USD	14,100	0.4
ETFS Gasoline	UGAS	B15KXW4	GB00B15KXW40	JE	USD	1,710	0.8
ETFS Heating Oil	HEAT	B15KXY6	GB00B15KXY63	JE	USD	2,440	0.7
ETFS Natural Gas	NGAS	B15KY10	GB00B15KY104	JE	USD	16,600,000	0.4
ETFS Natural Gas	NGSP	B285YS6	GB00B15KY104		GBP	244,000	0.2
ETFS Brent	OILB	B0CTWC0	GB00B0CTWC01	JE	USD	113,000	0.8
ETFS Brent	OLBP	B286069	GB00B0CTWC01		GBP	4,340	0.7
ETFS Brent 1yr	OSB1	B1YN4R6	JE00B1YN4R61	JE	USD	10,400	0.6
ETFS Brent 2yr	OSB2	B1YNWG1	JE00B1YNWG12	JE	USD	177	0.5
ETFS Brent 3yr	OSB3	B1YP740	JE00B1YP7409	JE	USD	852	0.4
ETFS WTI 1yr	OSW1	B1YPB60	JE00B1YPB605	JE	USD	1,390	0.8
ETFS WTI 2yr	OSW2	B1YPB71	JE00B1YPB712	JE	USD	397	0.6
ETFS WTI 3yr	OSW3	B1YPB93	JE00B1YPB936	JE	USD	153	0.5
ETFS WTI 2mth	OILW	B0CTWK8	GB00B0CTWK84	JE	USD	60,900	0.8
ETFS WTI 2mth	OLWP	B2860J2	GB00B0CTWK84		GBP	4,810	0.8

Source: Sharescope, London Stock Exchange

Table 1b: Leveraged energy commodities

ETF	TIDM	SEDOL	ISIN	Country of ETF Registration	Price Currency	Average Daily Volume	Beta
ETFS Leveraged Crude Oil	LOIL	B2NFTJ7	JE00B2NFTJ73	JE	USD	1,780,000	2.7
ETFS Leveraged Gasoline	LGAS	B2NFTK8	JE00B2NFTK88	JE	USD	9,240	2.2
ETFS Leveraged Heating Oil	LHEA	B2NFTM0	JE00B2NFTM03	JE	USD	4,550	1.8
ETFS Leveraged Natural Gas	LNGA	B2NFTQ4	JE00B2NFTQ41	JE	USD	1,610,000	0.4

Source: Sharescope, London Stock Exchange

Table 1c: Short energy commodities

ETF	TIDM	SEDOL	ISIN	Country of ETF Registration	Price Currency	Average Daily Volume	Beta
ETFS Short Crude Oil	SOIL	B24DK97	JE00B24DK975	JE	USD	75,100	-1.2
ETFS Short Gasoline	SGAS	B24DKB9	JE00B24DKB91	JE	USD	700	-1.0
ETFS Short Heating Oil	SHEA	B24DKD1	JE00B24DKD16	JE	USD	540	-0.9
ETFS Short Natural Gas	SNGA	B24DKH5	JE00B24DKH53	JE	USD	8,550	-0.5

Source: Sharescope, London Stock Exchange

Table 2a: Energy indices

ETF	TIDM	SEDOL	ISIN	Country of ETF Registration	Price Currency	Average Daily Volume	Beta
ETFS Energy DJ-UBSCI(SM)	AIGE	B15KYB0	GB00B15KYB02	JE	USD	50,300	0.7
ETFS Petroleum DJ-UBSCI(SM)	AIGO	B15KYC1	GB00B15KYC19	JE	USD	11,500	0.8

Source: Sharescope, London Stock Exchange

Table 2b: Forward energy indices

ETF	TIDM	SEDOL	ISIN	Country of ETF Registration	Price Currency	Average Daily Volume	Beta
ETFS Forward Energy DJ-UBSCI-F3(SM)	ENEF	B24DMD5	JE00B24DMD55	JE	USD	880	0.7
ETFS Forward Petroleum DJ-UBSCI-F3(SM)	FPET	B24DMF7	JE00B24DMF79	JE	USD	91	0.9

Source: Sharescope, London Stock Exchange

Table 2c: Leveraged energy indices

ETF	TIDM	SEDOL	ISIN	Country of ETF Registration	Price Currency	Average Daily Volume	Beta
ETFS Leveraged Energy DJ-UBSCI(SM)	LNRG	B2NFT53	JE00B2NFT534	JE	USD	2,350	1.7
ETFS Leveraged Petroleum DJ-UBSCI(SM)	LPET	B2NFT97	JE00B2NFT971	JE	USD	4,130	2.1

Source: Sharescope, London Stock Exchange

Table 2c: Short energy indices

ETF	TIDM	SEDOL	ISIN	Country of ETF Registration	Price Currency	Average Daily Volume	Beta
ETFS Short Energy DJ-UBSCI(SM)	SNRG	B24DKV9	JE00B24DKV97	JE	USD	123	-0.9
ETFS Short Petroleum DJ-UBSCI(SM)	SPET	B24DKW0	JE00B24DKW05	JE	USD	399	-1.1

Source: Sharescope, London Stock Exchange

Table 3: Energy-related stock indices

ETF	TIDM	SEDOL	ISIN	Country of ETF Registration	Price Currency	Average Daily Volume	Beta
db x-trackers DJ STOXX 600 Oil & Gas	XSER	B39DX90	LU0292101796	LU	GBP	1,470	1.9
db x-trackers DJ STOXX 600 Oil & Gas Short	XSES	B39DWV5	LU0322249623	LU	GBP	3,000	-1.8
ETFX DJ Stoxx 600 Oil & Gas	OILG	B3CJYS1	IE00B3CNH840	IE	EUR	3,650	1.7
ETFX DJ Stoxx 600 Oil & Gas	OILS	B3DWS65	IE00B3CNH840		GBP	1,400	1.7
PowerShares Gbl Clean Energy Fund	PSBW	B248K14	IE00B23D9133	IE	GBP	5,340	1.4

Source: Sharescope, London Stock Exchange

2. Precious Metals

Table 4a: Precious metal commodities

ETF	TIDM	SEDOL	ISIN	Country of ETF Registration	Price Currency	Average Daily Volume	Beta
ETFS Gold	BULL	B15KXX5	GB00B15KXX56	JE	USD	110,000	0.1
ETFS Gold	BULP	B285Z05	GB00B15KXX56		GBP	17,700	-0.2
ETFS Physical Gold	PHAU	B1VS377	JE00B1VS3770	JE	USD	131,000	0.1
ETFS Physical Gold	PHGP	B285Z72	JE00B1VS3770		GBP	9,100	-0.2
ETFS Physical Palladium	PHPD	B1VS300	JE00B1VS3002	JE	USD	39,700	0.8
ETFS Physical Platinum	PHPT	B1VS2W5	JE00B1VS2W53	JE	USD	25,900	0.5
ETFS Physical Silver	PHAG	B1VS333	JE00B1VS3333	JE	USD	128,000	0.6
ETFS Physical Silver	PHSP	B285ZK5	JE00B1VS3333		GBP	8,620	0.3
ETFS Silver	SLVR	B15KY32	GB00B15KY328	JE	USD	97,800	0.6
Lyxor Gold Bullion Securities Ltd	GBS	B00FHZ8	GB00B00FHZ82	JE	USD	259,000	0.1
Lyxor Gold Bullion Securities Ltd	GBSS	B291NZ3	GB00B00FHZ82		GBP	12,200	-0.2

Source: Sharescope, London Stock Exchange

Table 4b: Leveraged precious metal commodities

ETF	TIDM	SEDOL	ISIN	Country of ETF Registration	Price Currency	Average Daily Volume	Beta
ETFS Leveraged Gold	LBUL	B2NFTL9	JE00B2NFTL95	JE	USD	25,100	0.6
ETFS Leveraged Platinum	LPLA	B2NFV13	JE00B2NFV134	JE	USD	13,600	0.3
ETFS Leveraged Silver	LSIL	B2NFTS6	JE00B2NFTS64	JE	USD	80,900	1.6

Source: Sharescope, London Stock Exchange

Table 4c: Short precious metal commodities

ETF	TIDM	SEDOL	ISIN	Country of ETF Registration	Price Currency	Average Daily Volume	Beta
ETFS Short Gold	SBUL	B24DKC0	JE00B24DKC09	JE	USD	11,600	-0.1
ETFS Short Platinum	SPLA	B2NFT19	JE00B2NFT195	JE	USD	1,040	-0.6
ETFS Short Silver	SSIL	B24DKK8	JE00B24DKK82	JE	USD	6,150	-0.8

Source: Sharescope, London Stock Exchange

Table 5a: Precious metal index

ETF	TIDM	SEDOL	ISIN	Country of ETF Registration	Price Currency	Average Daily Volume	Beta
ETFS Precious Metals DJ-UBSCI(SM)	AIGP	B15KYF4	GB00B15KYF40	JE	USD	54,700	0.2

Source: Sharescope, London Stock Exchange

Table 5b: Leveraged precious metal index

ETF	TIDM	SEDOL	ISIN	Country of ETF Registration	Price Currency	Average Daily Volume	Beta
ETFS Leveraged Precious Metals DJ-UBSCI(SM)	LPMT	B2NFV79	JE00B2NFV795	JE	USD	7,330	0.6

Source: Sharescope, London Stock Exchange

Table 5c: Short precious metal index

ETF	TIDM	SEDOL	ISIN	Country of ETF Registration	Price Currency	Average Daily Volume	Beta
ETFS Short Precious Metals DJ-UBSCI(SM)	SPMT	B24DKY2	JE00B24DKY29	JE	USD	1,220	-0.3

Source: Sharescope, London Stock Exchange

Table 6: Precious metal-related stock indices

ETF	TIDM	SEDOL	ISIN	Country of ETF Registration	Price Currency	Average Daily Volume	Beta
ETFX Russell Global Gold	AUCO	B3CJVD5	IE00B3CNHG25	IE	USD	16,200	1.3
ETFX Russell Global Gold	AUCP	B3DWRM4	IE00B3CNHG25		GBP	8,020	1.2

Source: Sharescope, London Stock Exchange

3. Industrial Metals

Table 7a: Industrial metal commodities

ETF	TIDM	SEDOL	ISIN	Country of ETF Registration	Price Currency	Average Daily Volume	Beta
ETFS Aluminium	ALUM	B15KXN5	GB00B15KXN58	JE	USD	81,600	0.5
ETFS Carbon	CARB	B3CG631	JE00B3CG6315	JE	Euro	1,650	1.0
ETFS Carbon	CARP	B3F3Z09	JE00B3CG6315		GBP	820	0.9
ETFS Copper	COPA	B15KXQ8	GB00B15KXQ89	JE	USD	22,000	1.2
ETFS Nickel	NICK	B15KY21	GB00B15KY211	JE	USD	15,800	0.1
ETFS Zinc	ZINC	B15KY87	GB00B15KY872	JE	USD	22,700	1.0

Source: Sharescope, London Stock Exchange

Table 7b: Leveraged industrial metal commodities

ETF	TIDM	SEDOL	ISIN	Country of ETF Registration	Price Currency	Average Daily Volume	Beta
ETFS Leveraged Aluminium	LALU	B2NFTC0	JE00B2NFTC05	JE	USD	7,280	1.0
ETFS Leveraged Copper	LCOP	B2NFTF3	JE00B2NFTF36	JE	USD	22,700	2.8
ETFS Leveraged Lead	LLEA	B2NFTZ3	JE00B2NFTZ32	JE	USD	7,050	1.6
ETFS Leveraged Nickel	LNIK	B2NFTR5	JE00B2NFTR57	JE	USD	15,800	2.2
ETFS Leveraged Tin	LTIM	B2NFV24	JE00B2NFV241	JE	USD	1,890	1.1
ETFS Leveraged Zinc	LZIC	B2NFTY2	JE00B2NFTY25	JE	USD	4,280	0.9

Source: Sharescope, London Stock Exchange

Table 7c: Short industrial metal commodities

ETF	TIDM	SEDOL	ISIN	Country of ETF Registration	Price Currency	Average Daily Volume	Beta
ETFS Short Aluminium	SALU	B24DK42	JE00B24DK421	JE	USD	632	-0.7
ETFS Short Copper	SCOP	B24DK64	JE00B24DK645	JE	USD	10,900	-1.4
ETFS Short Lead	SLEA	B2NFT08	JE00B2NFT088	JE	USD	275	-0.9
ETFS Short Nickel	SNIK	B24DKJ7	JE00B24DKJ77	JE	USD	372	-1.0
ETFS Short Tin	STIM	B2NFT20	JE00B2NFT203	JE	USD	264	-0.7
ETFS Short Zinc	SZIC	B24DKS6	JE00B24DKS68	JE	USD	754	-1.0

Source: Sharescope, London Stock Exchange

Table 8a: Industrial metal indices

ETF	TIDM	SEDOL	ISIN	Country of ETF Registration	Price Currency	Average Daily Volume	Beta
ETFS Forward Industrial Metals DJUBSCIF3(SM)	FIND	B24DMJ1	JE00B24DMJ18	JE	USD	1,190	0.9
ETFS Industrial Metals DJ-UBSCI(SM)	AIGI	B15KYG5	GB00B15KYG56	JE	USD	111,000	0.2
ETFS Metal PM	PHPM	B1VS3W2	JE00B1VS3W29	JE	USD	3,090	0.2
ETFS Metal PM	PHPP	B285ZX8	JE00B1VS3W29		GBP	1,360	0.0

Source: Sharescope, London Stock Exchange

Table 8b: Leveraged industrial metal index

ETF	TIDM	SEDOL	ISIN	Country of ETF Registration	Price Currency	Average Daily Volume	Beta
ETFS Leveraged Industrial Metal DJ-UBSCI(SM)	LIME	B2NFV68	JE00B2NFV688	JE	USD	4,330	-0.3

Source: Sharescope, London Stock Exchange

Table 8c: Short industrial metal index

ETF	TIDM	SEDOL	ISIN	Country of ETF Registration	Price Currency	Average Daily Volume	Beta
ETFS Short Industrial Metals DJ-UBSCI(SM)	SIME	B24DKZ3	JE00B24DKZ36	JE	USD	2,060	-1.0

Source: Sharescope, London Stock Exchange

4. Agriculture

Table 9a: Agriculture commodities

ETF	TIDM	SEDOL	ISIN	Country of ETF Registration	Price Currency	Average Daily Volume	Beta
ETFS Coffee	COFF	B15KXP7	GB00B15KXP72	JE	USD	145,000	0.5
ETFS Corn	CORN	B15KXS0	GB00B15KXS04	JE	USD	630,000	0.8
ETFS Cotton	COTN	B15KXT1	GB00B15KXT11	JE	USD	128,000	0.6
ETFS Forward Lean Hogs	HOGF	B24DM13	JE00B24DM138	JE	USD	1,130	0.3
ETFS Forward Live Cattle	CATF	B24DM24	JE00B24DM245	JE	USD	315	0.4
ETFS Lean Hogs	HOGS	B15KXZ7	GB00B15KXZ70	JE	USD	161,000	0.2
ETFS Live Cattle	CATL	B15KY09	GB00B15KY096	JE	USD	8,530	0.3
ETFS Soybean Oil	SOYO	B15KY43	GB00B15KY435	JE	USD	8,840	0.6
ETFS Soybeans	SOYB	B15KY54	GB00B15KY542	JE	USD	23,700	0.6
ETFS Sugar	SUGA	B15KY65	GB00B15KY658	JE	USD	80,200	0.5
ETFS Wheat	WEAT	B15KY76	GB00B15KY765	JE	USD	686,000	0.5

Source: Sharescope, London Stock Exchange

Table 9b: Leveraged agriculture commodities

ETF	TIDM	SEDOL	ISIN	Country of ETF Registration	Price Currency	Average Daily Volume	Beta
ETFS Leveraged Cocoa	LCOC	B2NFV80	JE00B2NFV803	JE	USD	4,040	1.2
ETFS Leveraged Coffee	LCFE	B2NFTD1	JE00B2NFTD12	JE	USD	8,980	0.9
ETFS Leveraged Corn	LCOR	B2NFTG4	JE00B2NFTG43	JE	USD	12,100	1.0
ETFS Leveraged Cotton	LCTO	B2NFTH5	JE00B2NFTH59	JE	USD	8,200	1.8
ETFS Leveraged Lean Hogs	LLHO	B2NFTN1	JE00B2NFTN10	JE	USD	6,570	0.3
ETFS Leveraged Live Cattle	LLCT	B2NFTP3	JE00B2NFTP34	JE	USD	687	0.7
ETFS Leveraged Soybean Oil	LSYO	B2NFTT7	JE00B2NFTT71	JE	USD	6,690	1.3
ETFS Leveraged Soybeans	LSOB	B2NFTV9	JE00B2NFTV93	JE	USD	8,220	1.3
ETFS Leveraged Sugar	LSUG	B2NFTW0	JE00B2NFTW01	JE	USD	12,900	1.4
ETFS Leveraged Wheat	LWEA	B2NFTX1	JE00B2NFTX18	JE	USD	21,700	1.7

Source: Sharescope, London Stock Exchange

Table 9c: Short agriculture commodities

ETF	TIDM	SEDOL	ISIN	Country of ETF Registration	Price Currency	Average Daily Volume	Beta
ETFS Short Cocoa	SCOC	B2NFT31	JE00B2NFT310	JE	USD	1,660	-0.5
ETFS Short Coffee	SCFE	B24DK53	JE00B24DK538	JE	USD	1,950	-0.6
ETFS Short Corn	SCOR	B24DK75	JE00B24DK751	JE	USD	2,190	-0.7
ETFS Short Cotton	SCTO	B24DK86	JE00B24DK868	JE	USD	1,520	-0.8
ETFS Short Lean Hogs	SLHO	B24DKF3	JE00B24DKF30	JE	USD	3,020	-0.2
ETFS Short Live Cattle	SLCT	B24DKG4	JE00B24DKG47	JE	USD	197	-0.3
ETFS Short Soybean Oil	SSYO	B24DKL9	JE00B24DKL99	JE	USD	1,050	-0.7
ETFS Short Soybeans	SSOB	B24DKP3	JE00B24DKP38	JE	USD	940	-0.6
ETFS Short Sugar	SSUG	B24DKQ4	JE00B24DKQ45	JE	USD	4,810	-0.8
ETFS Short Wheat	SWEA	B24DKR5	JE00B24DKR51	JE	USD	2,920	-0.7

Source: Sharescope, London Stock Exchange

Table 10a: Agriculture indices

ETF	TIDM	SEDOL	ISIN	Country of ETF Registration	Price Currency	Average Daily Volume	Beta
ETFS Agriculture DJ-UBSCI(SM)	AIGA	B15KYH6	GB00B15KYH63	JE	USD	684,000	0.7
ETFS Agriculture DJ-UBSCI(SM)	AGAP	B285XZ6	GB00B15KYH63		GBP	53,200	0.3
ETFS Grains DJ-UBSCI(SM)	AIGG	B15KYL0	GB00B15KYL00	JE	USD	60,100	0.7
ETFS Grains DJ-UBSCI(SM)	AGGP	B285YH5	GB00B15KYL00		GBP	2,680	0.5
ETFS Livestock DJ-UBSCI(SM)	AIGL	B15KYK9	GB00B15KYK92	JE	USD	104,000	0.2
ETFS Softs DJ-UBSCI(SM)	AIGS	B15KYJ8	GB00B15KYJ87	JE	USD	63,200	0.5

Source: Sharescope, London Stock Exchange

Table 10b: Forward agriculture indices

ETF	TIDM	SEDOL	ISIN	Country of ETF Registration	Price Currency	Average Daily Volume	Beta
ETFS Forward Agriculture DJ-UBSCI-F3(SM)	FAGR	B24DMK2	JE00B24DMK23	JE	USD	16,800	0.7
ETFS Forward Grains DJ-UBSCI-F3(SM)	GRAF	B24DMN5	JE00B24DMN53	JE	USD	29,200	0.8
ETFS Forward Livestock DJ-UBSCI-F3(SM)	FLIV	B24DMM4	JE00B24DMM47	JE	USD	220	0.3
ETFS Forward Softs DJ-UBSCI-F3(SM)	SOFF	B24DML3	JE00B24DML30	JE	USD	1,640	0.6

Source: Sharescope, London Stock Exchange

Table 10c: Leveraged agriculture indices

ETF	TIDM	SEDOL	ISIN	Country of ETF Registration	Price Currency	Average Daily Volume	Beta
ETFS Leveraged Agriculture DJ-UBSCI(SM)	LAGR	B2NFT42	JE00B2NFT427	JE	USD	3,590	1.3
ETFS Leveraged Grains DJ-UBSCI(SM)	LGRA	B2NFT75	JE00B2NFT757	JE	USD	4,710	1.6
ETFS Leveraged Livestock DJ-UBSCI(SM)	LLST	B2NFT86	JE00B2NFT864	JE	USD	761	0.4
ETFS Leveraged Softs DJ-UBSCI(SM)	LSFT	B2NFTB9	JE00B2NFTB97	JE	USD	2,610	1.4

Source: Sharescope, London Stock Exchange

Table 10d: Short agriculture indices

ETF	TIDM	SEDOL	ISIN	Country of ETF Registration	Price Currency	Average Daily Volume	Beta
ETFS Short Agriculture DJ-UBSCI(SM)	SAGR	B24DL05	JE00B24DL056	JE	USD	106	-0.7
ETFS Short Grains DJ-UBSCI(SM)	SGRA	B24DL38	JE00B24DL387	JE	USD	142	-0.7
ETFS Short Livestock DJ-UBSCI(SM)	SLST	B24DL27	JE00B24DL270	JE	USD	116	-0.3
ETFS Short Softs DJ-UBSCI(SM)	SSFT	B24DL16	JE00B24DL163	JE	USD	1,000	-0.7

Source: Sharescope, London Stock Exchange

Table 11: Agriculture-related stock indices

ETF	TIDM	SEDOL	ISIN	Country of ETF Registration	Price Currency	Average Daily Volume	Beta
ETFX S-Net ITG Global Agri Business	AGRI	B3CJV46	IE00B3CNHD93	IE	USD	3,010	1.6
ETFX S-Net ITG Global Agri Business	AGRP	B3DWRH9	IE00B3CNHD93		GBP	622	1.3
PowerShares Global Agriculture Fund	PSGA	B3CBT82	IE00B3BQ0418	IE	GBP	5,170	1.3

Source: Sharescope, London Stock Exchange

5. Miscellaneous indices

Table 12a: Miscellaneous indices

ETF	TIDM	SEDOL	ISIN	Country of ETF Registration	Price Currency	Average Daily Volume	Beta
ETFS All Commodities DJ-UBSCI(SM)	AIGC	B15KY98	GB00B15KY989	JE	USD	50,300	0.6
ETFS All Commodities DJ-UBSCI(SM)	AGCP	B285Y75	GB00B15KY989		GBP	1,920	0.4
ETFS Ex-Energy DJ-UBSCI(SM)	AIGX	B15KYD2	GB00B15KYD26	JE	USD	3,990	0.6
Lyxor ETF CRB (Reuters/Jeff)	LCTY	B1YZPF7	FR0010455485	FR	GBP	13,900	0.3
Lyxor ETF CRB (Reuters/Jeff)	LCTU	B1Z2RL7	FR0010455485		USD	9,780	0.7
Lyxor ETF CRB Non-Energy (Reuters/Jeff)	LCNU	B1Z2RQ2	FR0010455493		USD	16,100	0.6
Lyxor ETF CRB Non-Energy (Reuters/Jeff)	LCNE	B1YZN86	FR0010455493	FR	GBP	3,400	0.3

Source: Sharescope, London Stock Exchange

Table 12b: Forward miscellaneous indices

ETF	TIDM	SEDOL	ISIN	Country of ETF Registration	Price Currency	Average Daily Volume	Beta
ETFS Forward All Commodities DJ-UBSCI-F3(SM)	FAIG	B24DMC4	JE00B24DMC49	JE	USD	20,400	0.6
ETFS Forward Ex-energy DJ-UBSCI-F3(SM)	EXEF	B24DMG8	JE00B24DMG86	JE	USD	108	0.6

Source: Sharescope, London Stock Exchange

Table 12c: Leveraged miscellaneous indices

ETF	TIDM	SEDOL	ISIN	Country of ETF Registration	Price Currency	Average Daily Volume	Beta
ETFS Leveraged All Commodities DJ-UBSCI(SM)	LALL	B2NFV57	JE00B2NFV571	JE	USD	4,270	1.4
ETFS Leveraged Ex-energy DJ-UBSCI(SM)	LNEY	B2NFT64	JE00B2NFT641	JE	USD	1,440	1.2

Source: Sharescope, London Stock Exchange

Table 12d: Short miscellaneous indices

ETF	TIDM	SEDOL	ISIN	Country of ETF Registration	Price Currency	Average Daily Volume	Beta
ETFS Short All Commodities DJ-UBSCI(SM))	SALL	B24DKT7	JE00B24DKT75	JE	USD	1,660	-0.7
ETFS Short Ex-energy DJ-UBSCI(SM)	SNEY	B24DKX1	JE00B24DKX12	JE	USD	0	-0.6

Source: Sharescope, London Stock Exchange

INDEX

A

agricultural commodities

corn 9, 117

demand 121-2

ETFs 22, 137, *see also* exchange traded funds (ETFs)

funds 138-9

oil and 119, 124

price history 119-121

soybeans and 117, 127, 128, 133, 135

supply 123

uses 119

vs. FTSE 100 120-1

wheat and 133, 134, 135

producers' reactions to prices 117

soybeans 117

biodiesel 127

corn and 117, 127, 128, 133, 135

demand 127-8

ETFs 22, 137, *see also* exchange traded funds (ETFs)

funds 138-9

price history 125-6, 129

supply 128

uses 125

vs. FTSE 100 126

wheat and 133, 134, 135

wheat 117

corn and 133, 134, 135

demand 133

ETFs 22, 137, *see also* exchange traded funds (ETFs)

funds 138-9

price history 131-3

soybeans and 133, 134, 135

supply 134-5

uses 131

vs. FTSE 100 133

aluminium, *see* industrial metals

automobile industry 61, 63, 66, 70, 75, 76, 87

Australia

stock exchange 18

supply of commodities 76, 90, 102, 131, 134

B

biodiesel, *see* biofuel

biofuel 9, 117, 119, 121, 122, 125, 127, 131, 134-5

bonds 17

Brazil 8, 85, 103, 128, *see also* BRICs

Brent Crude oil 3

BRICs 8, 17, 85, 89, 103

C

China 75, 91, *see also* BRICs

demand for commodities 2, 5, 8-9, 33, 36, 41, 57, 70, 89, 95, 101, 107, 121, 127, 133

supply of commodities 76, 90, 108, 123, 134

commodities

baskets 22

correlation with inflation, 5, 11, 53, 59

correlation with other assets

bonds 5, 53

equities 2-3, 7, 86

index of prices 6, 7

investment methods 13-23

physical commodities 13-14, 79-80

overall outlook 11

risk 22

commodity super cycle 1

corn, *see* agricultural commodities

copper, *see* industrial metals

currency exposure 20-1

D

Deutsche Bank 17

direct investment in physical commodities 13-14, 79-80

diversification 18, 29

E

emerging markets 2, 5, 8, 9, 58

demand for commodities 33, 41, 57, 70, 85, 93, 95-6

emissions, *see* environment

energy commodities

natural gas

copper and 97

demand 41-2

ETFs 22, 45, 146-9, *see also* exchange traded funds (ETFs)

funds 46

oil and 39, 40, 41, 42, 43

price history 40-1

supply 42-3

uses 39

volatility 40

vs. FTSE 100 41

oil 30, 31, 33

corn and 119-120, 122

correlation with equities 29

demand 33-4, 36

ETFs 22, 45, *see also* exchange traded funds (ETFs)

exposure through other investments 29

funds 46-47

peak oil 34

Other great investing titles from
Harriman House

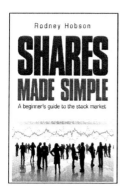

Shares Made Simple
A beginner's guide to the stock market
Rodney Hobson

Understanding Company News
How to interpret stock market announcements
Rodney Hobson

CFDs Made Simple
A straightforward guide to contracts for difference
Peter Temple

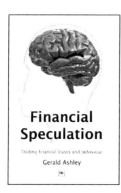

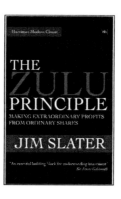

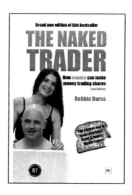

Financial Speculation
Trading financial biases and behaviour
Gerald Ashley

The Zulu Principle
Making extraordinary profits from ordinary shares
Jim Slater

The Naked Trader, 2nd edition
How anyone can make money trading shares
Robbie Burns

 Harriman House